Essential Websites for Educational Leaders in the 21st Century

James Lerman

ScarecrowEducation
Lanham, Maryland • Toronto • Oxford
2004

53986680

Published in the United States of America
by ScarecrowEducation
An imprint of The Rowman & Littlefield Publishing Group, Inc.
4501 Forbes Boulevard, Suite 200, Lanham, Maryland 20706
www.scarecroweducation.com

PO Box 317
Oxford
OX2 9RU, UK

British Library Cataloguing in Publication Information Available

Library of Congress Cataloging-in-Publication Data

Lerman, James, 1946–
  Essential Websites for educational leaders in the 21st century / James
Lerman.
    p. cm.
  ISBN 1-57886-130-6 (pbk. : alk. paper)
  1. Education—Computer network resources—Directories. 2. School
management and organization—Computer network resources—Directories.
3. Web sites—Directories. I. Title: Essential Websites for 21st-century
educational leaders. II. Title.
LB1044.87.L45 2004
371.2'00285—dc22

                                                           2004000009

Dedicated to the lights of my life,
Terry and Michela

Contents

Introduction

ARE YOU AN EDUCATIONAL LEADER? YES!

Chances are, if you are reading this, you care about education and are trying to improve it. In this writer's mind, that makes you an educational leader.

Educational leaders are people who care deeply about teaching and learning and who work, often very, very hard, to make the enterprise function more effectively. It does not matter what your role is in education. You may be a teacher, parent, student, school board member, principal, assistant principal, department head, consultant, central office staffer, college faculty member, concerned community person, elected official, graduate student, superintendent, state educational department staffer, representative of a federal or nonprofit agency—or you may wear more than one of these hats simultaneously.

No matter what hat you wear, as an educational leader, you have one main goal: to improve our students' education.

WHY YOU NEED THIS BOOK

As someone striving to improve education, you have two great needs:

1. You need a lot of reliable information, and
2. You need it at your fingertips . . . fast!

You know the Internet can help meet your needs. In fact, you know it was made for you—a total world of electronic information and tools at your personal beck and call. Trouble is, you do not have the time to sift through thousands of websites, even with the aid of a good search engine, to find just what you need. And you want to make sure that the information you find is from a source you can trust. At one time or another, you have probably wished that the key information you needed was just easier to get hold of, that someone would do the heavy sifting for you and pick out the best spots.

That is the purpose of this book: to identify the web's essential sites for you and help you get to them quickly. Whether you need policy research, data on school expenditures or student achievement, a free online career assessment inventory, instruction for third graders on how to use the net, lesson plans in advanced placement physics, sources for grants, a free service giving answers to your personal research questions, help in getting preschoolers ready to read, online videos of exemplary teaching, objective reviews of standardized tests or educational software, a free online collaborative workspace, or exercises for elementary students to practice their spelling, you will find current, relevant, and reliable information through the websites listed here.

MAKE THIS BOOK WORK FOR YOU

Essential Websites for Educational Leaders in the 21st Century is organized into 25 sections, each one listed in the table of contents. The sections were selected based on meticulous research into the wide variety of information requirements of educational leaders. Within each section, the chosen websites are found in alphabetical order, by name. The URL, or website address, is provided, and the strongest features and highlights of each site are described so you can decide if the information you are seeking is likely to be found there.

As you can see, *Essential Websites* operates primarily as a reference. It may be a good idea to browse through different sections of the book from time to time to obtain an overview of what it contains. This is especially true because all the selected websites do not always fit easily into one of the categories. What seems to you to be a policy question might be addressed in "School Administration"; what seems to be a curriculum resource might be located in "Teaching Resources." Nevertheless, *Essential Websites* will definitely be of greatest use to you at the very moment you need to find an answer to a question.

USE THE CD-ROM FOR SPEED AND CONVENIENCE

You will find a complete list of websites contained on the enclosed CD-ROM. The CD-ROM is in Adobe Acrobat format and should be readable by all computers that have the free Acrobat Reader installed, both PCs and Macs. If for some reason Acrobat Reader is not installed on your computer, you may download it for free from this site: www.adobe.com /products/acrobat/readstep2.html.

When you run the CD-ROM, you will find that you can jump from a listing in the table of contents directly to that section in the body of the text. For example, if you want to go to the "Personal Productivity" section, just click on it in the table of contents and you will be taken to the beginning of that area in the book. You will also find that, while on the CD-ROM, if you place your cursor over the blue URL for a site, you can click on it and be taken directly to that website on the Internet.

After you use the CD-ROM a couple of times, you will probably find this to be a much easier and faster way to locate the information you want. No more typing in long URL addresses and then having to check them, character by character, to make sure you have done it correctly. Just insert the CD-ROM and surf to your heart's content.

HOW THE SITES WERE CHOSEN

Many, many resources were consulted in assembling the collection found in *Essential Websites*. These include professional magazines, books, websites of organizations that present awards for outstanding online resources, conference presentations, recommendations by colleagues, compilations of outstanding sites by individuals and organizations, and numerous searches using a variety of search engines.

In order to make it into the book, a site had to demonstrate:

1. Ease of access
2. Content of value
3. Ease of navigation
4. Credibility/reliability of content
5. Relevance for the reader

When more than one website addressed itself to the same topic, the site or sites that were the best at what they did (in the author's opinion) were the ones chosen. And last, but far from least, the site must be free of charge. Sites that charge money are not included, except in a very few cases where they are included by reference only.

ERIC CLEARINGHOUSE SITES SUPPORTED BY THE FEDERAL GOVERNMENT

In December 2003, federal support for the system of ERIC Clearing-houses came to an end. A number of these Clearinghouses have been selected for inclusion in this volume. All of them have served as valuable sources of information in their respective areas. The U.S. Department of Education has announced that it is supporting a new system of gathering and reporting educational research. At this writing, the system is still in its formative stages and has yet to appear to the public.

Most of the Clearinghouses have moved their archives to new spots on the web. These new locations may not have all of the functionality of the former locations. Readers may access the Clearinghouse information in two ways: (1) Listed in the following text are the new URLs for the Clear-inghouses. (2) Using the Wayback Machine website, at webdev.archive .org/index.php, readers may access archived versions of the old Clearing-houses (see chapter 22, item 22.7 for a further description of the Wayback Machine.)

The following information is from the January 14, 2004, issue of *Education Week,* which cites the source as Cheryl Grossman, from the Center on Education and Training for Employment at Ohio State University.

Shown first is the name of the former ERIC Clearinghouse, then the URL for its archived information.

Clearinghouse on Adult, Career, and Vocational Education: www.cete.org/acve; www-tcall.tamu.edu/erica

Clearinghouse on Assessment and Evaluation: edresearch.org

Clearinghouse for Community Colleges: None

Clearinghouse on Counseling and Student Services: www.counselingoutfitters.com

Clearinghouse on Disabilities and Gifted Education: www.cec.sped.org

Clearinghouse on Educational Management: cepm.uoregon.edu

Clearinghouse on Elementary and Early Childhood Education: ecap.crc.uiuc.edu/info

Clearinghouse on Information and Technology: www.eduref.org

Clearinghouse on Higher Education: None

Clearinghouse on Languages and Linguistics: www.cal.org

Clearinghouse on Reading, English, and Communications: www.kidscanlearn.com

Clearinghouse on Rural Education and Small Schools: www.aelc.org

Clearinghouse on Science, Mathematics, and Environmental Education: stemworks.org

Clearinghouse for Social Studies/Social Science Education: www.indiana.edu/~ssdc/ssdc.htm

Clearinghouse on Teaching and Teacher Education: www.aacte.org

Clearinghouse on Urban Education: iume.tc.columbia.edu

FINAL WORDS ABOUT ACCURACY OF WEBSITE ADDRESSES AND SITES THAT DISAPPEAR

Every website address (URL) included in *Essential Websites* was checked for accuracy just prior to the book's publication. Unfortunately, it is a fact of life on the web that change is constant. Sites that may be here today are gone tomorrow, with a new name or location, or they may have just disappeared into the ether. It can be quite frustrating.

One way to locate sites that have disappeared is to type the name of the site into a search engine such as Google or Yahoo. The search engine may locate the site's new URL. Another way is to use the Wayback Machine located at webdev.archive.org/index.php. If you go to item 22.7 in this book, you will locate information that tells you how to use this wonderful resource. More than half the time I have used the Wayback Machine, I have been able to find the site that left without a trace.

Putting *Essential Websites* together has been a rewarding learning experience. I am grateful to ScarecrowEducation for giving me the opportunity to share this information. I hope you find it useful.

James Lerman

Chapter One

Assessment

1.1 CRESST—National Center for Research on Evaluation, Standards, and Student Testing
www.cresst96.cse.ucla.edu

CRESST focuses on assessment and evaluation. The site contains online research reports, archived newsletters, PowerPoint slides from conference presentations, a separate section for parents, and its newest online package called "Quality School Portfolio: Using Data to Improve Student Performance."

1.2 Digital Resources for Evaluators
www.resources4evaluators.info

Here is one-stop shopping for links to resources on evaluation. I especially like the section "Most Used or Favorite Sites," which links to more than a dozen of the most helpful resources on evaluation. Other sections include "Communities of Evaluators"; "Education and Training in Evaluation"; "Government Agencies, Foundations, and Organizations"; "Companies and Consultants"; "Evaluation Texts and Documents"; "Instruments, Data, Surveys, Statistics, and Software"; and "Funding and Employment."

1.3 ETS Test Locator
www.ets.org/testcoll/index.html

If it is information about specific tests you are looking for, this is a great place to begin. Educational Testing Service has assembled a collection of more than "20,000 tests and other measurement devices from the early

1900's to the present." The service is a searchable database that yields descriptions of tests and instruments. Once you have found tests of interest, you may order them in microfiche, download the limited number available in Adobe Acrobat format, or order directly from the publisher.

1.4   FairTest—National Center for Fair and Open Testing
www.fairtest.org

FairTest describes itself as "an advocacy organization working to end the abuses, misuses, and flaws of standardized testing and ensure that evaluation of students and workers is fair, open, and educationally sound." The site links to many relevant articles in support of this point of view, publishes more than two dozen Fact Sheets on significant issues in K–12 and university testing, provides a home to the Assessment Reform Network, hosts a discussion board, and posts news items on a frequent basis.

1.5   RubiStar
rubistar.4teachers.org

This free site provides an online tool to construct rubrics. The focus is on projects in nine subject areas, K–12. After assessment using a rubric, data can be entered into RubiStar to yield a class profile.

1.6   Students Against Testing
www.nomoretests.com

Founded by Bill Wetzel, the site spearheads a movement of sorts. Wetzel, a very intelligent and fortunate young man from New Jersey, has been both the author and subject of articles in *Teacher* magazine. Now in his early 20s, after a few years' traveling about the United States after high school, he presently attends NYU and is writing a book. The site encourages people, particularly students, to take action against standardized tests and provides a toolkit for doing so. It contains extensive links to articles, research, quotations, and a soon-promised discussion board.

Chapter Two

Community Relations

2.1 Communities at Work: A Guidebook of Strategic Interventions for Community Change
www.publiceducation.org/pdf/CAW/CAW_report.pdf

This online version of a 66-page volume focuses on the roles of Local Education Funds (LEFs) in promoting systemic improvements in schools. There are 66 LEFs officially affiliated with the Public Education Network (PEN), publisher of the report, and many more local groups across the nation who may be unconnected to PEN but share its general goals. The guide focuses on key interventions that organizations may undertake to improve schools in their communities: "Community Dialogue," "Constituency Building," "Engaging Practitioners," "Collaborating with Districts," "Analyzing Policy," and "Following Legal Strategies." Each intervention is described, and examples undertaken by local groups are detailed. Lessons learned from these efforts and sample tools for implementation are also provided. Finally, each section offers references for additional information.

2.2 Communities in Schools (CIS)
www.cisnet.org

CIS is a specific program founded by William Milliken, focused on "helping kids prepare for life." The basics of CIS include: "A Personal Relationship with a Caring Adult," "A Safe Place" (after-school and extended-hours programs), "A Healthy Spot," "A Marketable Skill," and "A Chance to Give Back." Interested readers are encouraged to contact CIS to organize a local program.

2.3   Family Involvement Network of Educators (FINE)
www.gse.harvard.edu/~hfrp/projects/fine.html

FINE gives outstanding support for planning, implementing, and eval-
uating partnerships among families, schools, and communities. Organized
by the Harvard Family Research Project, FINE contains terrific bibliographies and research on school, family, and community issues. It provides
very detailed course syllabi from 18 different university courses on family involvement. You will also find many teaching cases to discuss, analyze, and reflect on, and a collection of excellent workshop materials for
training and presentation purposes.

2.4   Inclusion
www.quasar.ualberta.ca/ddc/incl/intro.htm#top

Inclusion practices and resources are highlighted at this site. Its cen-
terpiece is the *Handbook*, divided into "Elementary" and "Secondary"
topics for teachers titled "You Are Not Alone," "Getting Organized," and
"In the Classroom." Also provided are extensive online resources involving strategies, useful forms, and curriculum suggestions and modifi-
cations. Readers of the *Handbook* will find convenient links from each
topic to relevant, full-text resources. Field interviews with students, administrators, and over 100 teachers are also provided, which provide
multiple points of view and many practical pointers from the University
of Alberta, Canada.

2.5   National Center for Family and Community Connections with Schools
www.sedl.org/connections/resources.html

The Southwest Education Development Laboratory has created this excellent collection of materials. The Resources portion of the site is organized into five sections: (1) Publications database of over 270 items; (2)
Research syntheses, published annually; (3) Annual satellite broadcasts;
(4) Research briefs on key concepts focused on family and community
connections with schools; and (5) After-school program resources for program development and staff training.

2.6   National Coalition for Parent Involvement in Education (NCPIE)
www.ncpie.org

NCPIE offers brief articles on establishing a framework for family involvement, policy guidelines, and descriptions of keys to success. The site

also provides an extensive list of resources for program implementation and research, some available online.

2.7   National Network of Partnership Schools
www.csos.jhu.edu/p2000/default.htm

NNPS reigns as the gold standard in resources for family and community involvement. Based on Joyce Epstein's outstanding work at Johns Hopkins University, this site provides an abundance of information. It presents a framework for activity, guidelines for action teams, planning and evaluation tools, information about budgeting and funding, and a 12-month planning guide. Do not miss the archived volume of *Promising Partnership Practices* and the "Type 2" newsletter. The site is also home to the Teachers Involve Parents in Schoolwork (TIPS) program. TIPS provides a very organized and systematic approach to involving teachers with families to promote more effective learning from homework. While it is possible to use only the free online materials, schools that are serious about building their family and community involvement programs will probably want to make some purchases and perhaps join the more than 900 other schools that have signed up to be members of the Network.

2.8   National School Public Relations Association
www.nspra.org/entry.htm

This site gives tips on starting a school public relations program and a selection of articles on school public relations. NSPR offers many excellent and informative materials for sale and publishes three solid, hardcopy newsletters. It also conducts annual contests to recognize exemplary school and district programs. The names of the winners are posted here with information on how to contact them in case you wish to learn about their great work.

2.9   Parent Involvement
www.pta.org/parentinvolvement/index.asp

This section of the National PTA's website offers terrific support and assistance in building successful home and school partnerships. Be sure to look at the National Standards page (based on Joyce Epstein's work at Johns Hopkins—in item 2.7) that provides standards statements, quality indicators, sample applications, articles on key aspects, action guidelines, project ideas, a bibliography, and numerous tools and worksheets. The material is available in both Spanish and English. Interested readers may purchase PTA's book on the subject, *Building Successful Partnerships: A Guide to Developing Parent and Family Involvement Programs*. In addition, the PTA conducts an annual Parent Involvement Schools of Excellence Certification program to recognize and foster exemplary work and commitment.

2.10   School-Family-Community Partnerships Team
www.nwrel.org/partnerships
A project of the Northwest Regional Education Laboratory, this group publishes five books, all available in full-text online. They are *Planning for Youth Success*, *Assessing Youth Success*, *Partnerships by Design*, *Building Relationships for Student Success*, and *Classroom to Community and Back*. The site also provides links to organizations, projects, and additional resources in the field.

2.11   The Knowledge Loom — School, Family, and Community Partnerships
knowledgeloom.org/practices3.jsp?location=1&bpinterid=1051& potlightid=1051
You will find this a very practical and t o-the-point spot for information. It is divided into five main topics: "Policies," "Leadership," "Communication," "Community," and "Evaluation." Within each topic, there are subsections containing a quick overview, at least one example of a successful practice, a research summary with references (some online), existing policy statements, and web resources for further information. The site is organized by the Education Alliance at Brown University.

Chapter Three

Crisis and Disaster Intervention

Sadly, the children and adults in our schools need support in dealing with issues of war, terrorism, violence, abuse, suicide, murder, catastrophic illness, untimely death, injury, and natural disasters far more often than it seems they should have to. While never being able to substitute for trained personnel, these sites can help before, during, and after crises, disasters, and other traumatic situations.

3.1   Available Free Resources—National Association of School Psychologists
www.nasponline.org/NEAT/resources.htm

This website contains an extensive list of 61 resources designed to help school psychologists and other officials establish school crisis teams and design crisis management plans. The links to crisis sites of many national organizations are particularly thorough. NASP has also organized a National Emergency Assistance Team (NEAT) that is available to help communities when a crisis strikes. Information on contacting a member of NEAT is available at www.nasponline.org/NEAT/contacts.html.

3.2   Centers for Disease Control and Prevention
www.cdc.gov

If your school or community is faced with the need for authoritative health information, particularly in a crisis situation, this is the first place you should go.

3.3   Disaster Response
www.aacap.org/publications/DisasterResponse/index.htm

The American Academy of Child and Adolescent Psychiatry has compiled this succinct list of 13 resources in English and Spanish to assist parents and children.

3.4   Help with the Healing, on the Web
www.connectforkids.org/resources3139/resources_show.htm?doc_id=
120823#Afterschocks
    Connect for Kids, the host of this site, describes itself as "Guidance for Grownups." The best qualities of this page are that (1) each of the 47 links comes with a brief description of what it leads to, and (2) it is organized into categories. The categories include "Helping Kids Cope with Trauma (General, Age Specific, and Loss and Grief)," "Guidance for Adults," "Anti-Discrimination Resources," and "Lesson Plans for Teachers."

3.5   Helping Children Cope with Tragedy
www.pta.org/parentinvolvement/tragedy/resources.asp
    Resources for Parents/Families from the National PTA consists of links to 17 websites and articles focused on crucial ways to assist parents and educators to help kids cope with these issues.

3.6   Plans to Analyze World Events, Wars, and Crises
www.esrnational.org/sp/we/world.htm
    Readers will find here a great many resources, lessons, guides, and best-of-web links organized into four categories: "Dealing with Crises and Teaching about Traumatic Events," "Understanding War," "Stopping Discrimination," and "Analyzing 9/11." Educators for Social Responsibility, a national nonprofit organization whose purpose is to make teaching social responsibility a core practice in education, maintains the site.

3.7   Resources for Helping Children Coping with Trauma and Loss
www.aboutourkids.org/articles/crisis_index.html
    These materials are published by the Child Study Center at New York University's School of Medicine. The page provides links to 28 articles for parents and teachers, including some in Spanish, focused on all aspects of trauma and loss, from the general to the specific. Two guides in the form of *Crisis Manuals* are available for download, and links are provided to the FEMA site for kids, Helping Children Handle Disaster-Related Anxiety, and the Institute for Trauma and Stress.

Chapter Four

Curriculum Resources

4.1   ARTSEDGE—The Kennedy Center
artsedge.kennedy-center.org/artsedge.html

"ARTSEDGE supports the place of arts education at the center of the curriculum." Toward that end, it offers an excellent collection of lessons and activities in the arts and also a large number of interdisciplinary plans in all other major subject areas. These materials are searchable by name, by grade level, and also through use of a power search feature. Extensive professional resources are given for educators and artists. I especially recommend the "How To's," "Guides," and "FAQs" sections which provide very practical guidance on topics such as coaching storytellers, playwriting with students, puppet making, photography, arts integration planning, and assessment in the arts.

Click the small hotlink near the bottom of the start page named "Sites We Host" to locate five more great arts sources.

4.2   ArtsEdNet
www.getty.edu/artsednet

For over a decade, the Getty Museum has advocated the use of discipline-based arts education as the best means for promoting fine arts learning. This interactive and well-designed site provides lesson plans and curriculum ideas, image galleries and exhibitions, and an active as well as archived online discussion group devoted to arts education.

4.3   Britannica Guide to Black History
search.eb.com/blackhistory

A comprehensive and exceptionally well-organized introduction to black history, aimed at students and teachers. It divides the history of people of African descent in the United States into five eras and provides an extensive timeline. Biographical articles and others on "Events and Institutions" are very well indexed, and a dozen audio and video clips of important events and people of the second half of the 20th century are provided. The selected Internet links and bibliography are all of high quality, as are a study guide for students and a teachers' guide contained within it. See also "African American Odyssey" at the Library of Congress: memory.loc.gov/ammem/aaohtml/exhibit/aointro.html.

4.4   Children's Literature Web Guide
www.ucalgary.ca/~dkbrown/

CLWG focuses on book-related resources for children and young adults, their parents, teachers, librarians, and book professionals. The site gathers a very well-organized collection of book reviews; links to discussion groups; full-text stories; resources for storytellers, writers, and illustrators; award-winning books; reader's theatre; authors' and illustrators' background information; and teaching ideas. CLWB is searchable and has won many awards.

4.5   Creating Music
www.creatingmusic.com

Creating Music allows anyone to actually make music online. Users can compose, edit, and hear their own compositions. A stated focus of the site is to familiarize users with the Euro-American tradition of writing music down. Exploration of this topic is pursued with games and activities that center on tempo and dynamics. Users also gain the experience of "conducting" by moving the mouse to control tempo. Additional exercises are promised in the future. This site is quite an amazing accomplishment.

4.6   Diversity
home.comcast.net/~dboals1/diversit.html

There is no other collection of links as extensive and well organized on this topic as Diversity. Each of the hundreds of links are organized into categories and described briefly. The categories are "General Sources," "The Cultural Landscape," "Electronic Communities," "Disabilities,"

"Migration and Immigration," "Asian-American Resources," "African-American Resources," "Hispanic/Latino Resources," "Jewish Resources," "Native American Resources," and "Women's Resources." Diversity is part of a much larger site, called the History/Social Studies Web Site for K–12 Teachers, that links to thousands of great resources. It is located at home.comcast.net/~dboals1/boals.html.

4.7 EconEdLink
www.econedlink.org/

The National Council on Economic Education has created this marvelously rich site to focus on web-based materials and strategies for teaching and learning about economics, K–12. Most online lessons can be completed in one period. Those contained in "EconomicsMinute" explore the relations between economics and real-world issues. "MillionaireMinute" centers on finance and financial planning. "NetNewsLine" explores the complex connections between current news and economics. Links to additional excellent educational resources, as well as real time economic data, are also provided.

4.8 EDSITEment
edsitement.neh.gov

The best of humanities education on the web, K–12, from the National Endowment for the Humanities. Main subjects include "Art & Culture," "Literature & Language Arts," "Foreign Language," and "History & Social Studies." Nearly 200 high quality units are included with extensive links to specific online source information for teachers and students. In addition, over 125 web links are given to sites offering educational materials and plans of their own. All resources are thoroughly described, and the site is organized to be very easy to search.

4.9 Eisenhower National Clearinghouse for Mathematics and Science Education
www.enc.org

ENC is extremely well organized and comprehensive; it is a leading educational portal. With a focus on math and science, it provides quality selected lesson plans and activities, professional resources, reference sources, student resources, websites on topical areas, and links to selected articles in eight key topic areas. ENC also publishes a comprehensive quarterly magazine, ENC Focus. Of particular note are the site's news pages, which provide daily updates on general education news, events, resources, and grants. You may also submit questions online and by telephone for reference searches for information, materials, and websites in math and science (see Ask ENC). Readers may register to have news bulletins and ENC Focus sent to them by e-mail.

4.10   English Language Acquisition and Language Instruction Educational Programs
www.ncela.gwu.edu
   Here is the first place to start when looking for information dealing with bilingual and ESL education. The site is user-friendly and searchable; see the easy index on the start page. It contains an extensive, full-text library, a large bibliographic database, links to hundreds of bilingual/ESL sites, lesson plans, success stories, and state resources. NCELA also maintains an active question line for e-mail users seeking more information.

4.11   Hispanic Heritage Teaching Resources
smithsonianeducation.org/educators/resource_library/hispanic_resources
.html
   This extraordinary collection of artistic, historic, and cultural resources spans the exceptional diversity of the Latino/a experience in North America. This page actually functions as a portal into multimedia explorations involving primarily Mexican and Puerto Rican peoples in their original settings as well as in their newer homes in the U.S. It contains a "Latino Virtual Gallery" incorporating "contributions to America's history, arts, and culture from a Latino/a perspective." Ten units include deep study of photography, fashion, aging, low riding, art, history, music, science, textiles, and letter writing. Bilingual material may be found throughout. While the units take Hispanic Heritage as a theme, they are indeed universal in their approach, so their use need not be limited to consideration of contributions by so-called minority groups.

4.12   iLoveLanguages
www.ilovelanguages.com
   Tyler Chambers has been compiling online resources about languages since 1994. This site now consists of over 2,000 personally selected links

organized into categories consisting of Languages, Schools, Commercial, Jobs, and New. The Language category contains subheadings titled "By Language," "Collections of Links," "Conferences," "Dictionaries," "Free Translation," "Language Lessons," "Linguistics," "Multilingual Resources," "Organizations," "Polish," and "Teaching Resources."

4.13   Jazz—A History of America's Music

www.pbs.org/jazz

Jazz is such a large topic that teaching about it can be a daunting task. But because jazz is America's music, it deserves serious study. In fact, Columbia University has recently included study of jazz as a required part of its undergraduate core curriculum. This website was developed to accompany Ken Burns's great PBS multipart documentary on jazz. It can be used on a stand-alone basis or in conjunction with the videos.

"Classroom" contains numerous creative lesson plans for elementary, middle, and high school students. The *General Motors Music Study Guide* contains (on the last page) an excellent guide to use when students listen to musical selections. Each of the entries in "Places, Spaces and Changing Faces" contains a minilesson, with audio clips, about the four main cities of jazz (New Orleans, Kansas City, Chicago, and New York), historically significant locations in them, and key trends in the development of jazz.

"Jazz Lounge" provides a brief overview of musical theory, audio samples of the major jazz styles for easy comparison, and even allows students to improvise their own compositions. At "Jazz in Time," you will find brief lessons, with audio clips, concerning the influence of historical events on the development of jazz at key junctures from the Civil War to the present day. A highlight of the "Musical Notes" section is inclusion of audio segments from nine of the most significant jazz songs in history. Biographies gives short bios of major jazz figures along with an audio clip of their work. "Jazz Exchange" supplies minilessons on key developments in popular culture and their influence on jazz.

4.14   KidsHealth

kidshealth.org

Divided into sections for kids, teens, and parents, this is the most visited website on young people's health information. It contains articles and interactive activities put together in kid-, teen-, and adult-friendly terms.

Some information is also available in Spanish, and readers may sign up for a weekly e-mail newsletter. Topics include "Staying Healthy," "Everyday Illnesses and Injuries," "My Body," "Staying Safe," and much more. KidsHealth is supported and maintained by the Nemours Foundation.

4.15   Language Links
polyglot.lss.wisc.edu/lss/lang/langlink.html

Lauren Rosen, at the University of Wisconsin, has assembled this great collection of material on teaching world (or foreign) languages. The first link on the home page takes you to "Teaching with the Web." It provides descriptions of sites that offer "Web Activities for Any Language," "Language Specific Activities," "Teaching Resources," "Collaborative Learning Activities," "Publications," and "Learning Centers and Associations." The second portion of the home page gives links to annotated sites focused on "Multi-Languages/All Languages," "African Languages and Literature," "Asian Studies," "Classics," "ESL/EFL," "French," "Germanic Languages," "Hebrew and Semitic Studies," "Italian," "Portuguese," "Quechua," "Scandinavian Studies," "Slavic," and "Spanish."

4.16   Naeg Center for Gifted Education and Talent Development
www.gifted.uconn.edu

Incorporating the National Research Center on the Gifted and Talented and its excellent biannual newsletter, this site describes several models for gifted education and now hosts the website for the national Accelerated Schools Project. Other useful resources are the conference handouts and PowerPoint presentations found at curry.edschool.virginia.edu/gifted/ projects/NRC/projects/projectinfo.html#current.

4.17   National Service-Learning Clearinghouse
www.servicelearning.org

Just as the name says, you will find here a U.S. government-supported, one-stop clearinghouse for information on service learning in higher education, K–12, community-based, and tribal settings. "The Library" links to online documents in 13 categories. "Resources and Tools" contains connections to "Tool Kits," "Syllabi and Curricula," "Funding Sources," "General Links," and a "Directory of Programs and Listservs." You can also find information about "Conferences and Events" as well as "Job Opportunities."

4.18   National Library of Virtual Manipulatives for Interactive Mathematics
matti.usu.edu/nlvm/enu/navd/index.html

Dozens of online, interactive mathematical manipulatives appear on NLVMIM, complete with lesson plans, connections to national standards, and detailed instructions for use of each workspace. Activities and materials are grouped by grade level (preK–2, 3–5, 6–8, 9–12) and by topic ("Number & Operations," "Algebra," "Geometry," "Measurement," and "Data Analysis & Probability"). New manipulatives are added periodically, all based on the NCTM standards. This is a truly outstanding application of technology to teaching—do not miss it. See also "Introduction to the World of Virtual Manipulatives" at www.paterson.k12.nj .us/%7Epps/math/mathstuff.htm for links to six more sites on virtual manipulatives.

4.19   NCTM Illuminations
illuminations.nctm.org

Lesson plans offer ready-to-go online activities developed and tested by expert teachers. More than 1,100 quality-reviewed online math resources are given, grouped by math topic and grade level. "Interactive Math Tools" illustrate many complex mathematical topics; they are very cool. "I-Math Investigations" include investigations for students, teacher's notes, answers, and related professional development activities. "Inquiry on Practice" is the professional development section, offering videos, interactive math content, research reports, and articles. All content may be viewed by grade level as well as the subject categories mentioned in the preceeding sentences. Despite its large size, Illuminations is easy to navigate.

4.20   PE Central
www.pecentral.org

Physical Education resources abound at PE Central, a location that has garnered over two dozen national awards for quality. The searchable site consists of 18 categories that contain original content, links, and items for purchase. Selected categories include "Lesson Plans," "Assessment Ideas," "Adapted Physical Education," "Preschool," "Creating a Positive Learning Climate," "Instructional Resources," "Research," and "Best Practices."

4.21   ReadWriteThink

www.readwritethink.org

This site, a collaboration between the International Reading Association and the National Council of Teachers of English, works to provide one-stop shopping for teachers and students to the best resources in language arts and reading. Extensive resources and tools are located here for grades K–12. ReadWriteThink is organized for easy navigation and provides "Lessons," "Standards," "Web Resources," three types of "Literacy Engagements," terrific "Student Materials," and a useful "Calendar." The "Web Resources" include "Instructional Resources," "Professional Development," and a "Reference Library." I especially like the "Comic Creator" ("Student Materials") that permits students to compose and critique their own comics online. Structured lessons facilitate this process for grades 3–12 and give powerful support for explorations of narrative structure, sequence, character development, and media stereotyping. Twenty-two additional powerful tools for students can also be found here.

4.22   Safe and Sound: An Education Leader's Guide to Evidence-Based Social and Emotional Learning (SEL) Programs

www.casel.org/projects_products/safeandsound.php

"Social and emotional learning (SEL) programs help reduce the achievement gap between high- and low-achieving youth by providing all students the necessary skills to be successful in school and life." These include self-awareness, social awareness, self-management, relationship skills, and responsible decision making. SEL is well supported by the American public in Gallup polls, by state legislators, and educators. This guide, published in March 2003, compiles data on 80 nationally available programs. It assesses them according to 14 criteria and identifies 22 as "'Select SEL Programs' that are especially effective and comprehensive in their SEL coverage, their documented impact, and the staff development they provide." Safe and Sound serves as an excellent guide to SEL program selection and is available for download from the website.

4.23   Science NetLinks

www.sciencenetlinks.com/index.cfm

Teachers and students will discover here a universe of the best resources for teaching and learning about science, K–12. The American Association for the Advancement of Science has collected lessons, tools, and resources in an easy-to-search format, all keyed to very clearly expressed science learning standards. More than 250 lessons are provided, with links to related lessons, many of them interactive on the computer or hands-on in class. Internet resources are carefully checked by AAAS's reviewer panel.

4.24 Special Education Resources on the Internet
seriweb.com

SERI works to gather into one place as much online information about special education as possible. It is divided into 23 sections and contains hundreds of briefly annotated links. Some of the topics include "Discussion Groups," "Physical and Health Disorders," "Special Needs and Technology," "Parents and Educators Resources," "Behavior Disorders," and "Transition Resources."

4.25 The Math Forum
mathforum.org

A simple way to start mining the many gems contained in Math Forum is to go to the "Quick Reference Page" (button located near the bottom of the home page). It features a matrix of quick links to the 32 areas within the overall site. Math Forum includes discussion spaces for math educators, model interactive projects for students (including six problem of the week services), educator-selected high-quality math and math education content, the "Internet Mathematics Library," "Ask Dr. Math," and access to a free e-mail newsletter. A truly outstanding resource for mathematics education.

4.26 Vocational Information Center
www.khake.com

Kathryn Hake has succeeded at a task that no think tank, university center, or foundation appears to have even attempted. She has created an up-to-date "central location for Career and Technical Education resources for students and education professionals." She has brought together as much online career and technical information as possible, organized it, and made it easy to find.

The start page begins with more than 90 categories of career topics and information sources. Other general categories are displayed at the bottom of the page, including career paths, tutorials, workforce skills, reference and search resources, information for educators, the job market, and an excellent site map as well as an index. Readers are taken to the best websites on each topic. This is an enormously practical and helpful collection of hotlinks.

4.27   Xpeditions
www.nationalgeographic.com/xpeditions

The U.S. geography standards serve as the foundation for this outstanding site from the National Geographic Society. Its main areas consist of "Activities," "Lesson Plans," "Xpedition Hall," and "Resources." The "Hall" functions as an interactive virtual museum, with imaginative exhibits illustrating each of the standards. "Activities" and "Lesson Plans" are organized similarly, by standard and by grade level. Resources include a fabulous, searchable collection of black-and-white maps for printing, discussion areas, a robust search function, and a blue-ribbon collection of links selected for the quality and depth of their geographic content.

Chapter Five

Education News

5.1 EducationNews.org
www.educationnews.org

This spot offers the most selected articles and links on a daily basis from around the country. It contains no advertising and also provides original content. Further, it gathers collections of links on topical issues and publishes a free, weekly e-zine.

5.2 Education Week on the Web
www.edweek.org

Education Week is the preeminent single location for news and information about American K–12 education. You will find all issues of the publication here, from the most recent, back to 1980. Everything is searchable.

"Daily News" includes headline links to education stories in the nation's leading daily newspapers. More links are included for journals, magazines, reports, and international education news from newspapers around the world. The full text of *Teacher* magazine appears here, as well as Education Week's well-known job advertisements. Also easily accessed are Education Week's "Special Reports," "Hot Topics" (well-researched reviews of major issues, with links to relevant news articles, reports, and websites), and the "State Info" section (a wealth of data on education in each state).

5.3 Education Headlines
www.enc.org/educationheadlines/?ls=ho

The Eisenhower National Clearinghouse culls daily news from 60 metropolitan dailies, two national newspapers, and three non-newspaper sources—including most of the nation's leading outlets. Readers may sign up to have this news delivered daily by e-mail.

5.4 Public Education Network Weekly NewsBlast
www.publiceducation.org/newsblast-current.asp

Here is a weekly e-zine available for subscription with over 40,000 recipients already logged on. *NewsBlast* summarizes the top education articles of the week as reported in the press and provides hotlinks to the full stories. Full-text reports of research studies as well as direct connections to relevant websites are included. In addition, *NewsBlast* offers an update on "Grants and Funding" in every issue and a "Quote of the Week."

5.5 Special Education News
www.specialednews.com

Devoted to daily news about special education, this site also maintains 12 bulletin boards for discussion and 11 article archives that contain links and reading lists.

Chapter Six

Educational Policy and Research

6.1   American Education Research Association—Journals
www.aera.net/pubs
  AERA, the preeminent education research organization in the world, publishes six journals. All copies are accessible through this site. The names of the journals are: *Educational Researcher*, *American Educational Research Journal*, *Education Evaluation and Policy Analysis*, *Journal of Educational and Behavioral Statistics*, *Review of Educational Research*, and *Review of Research in Education*. Some journals wait approximately six months before archiving their articles on the site; accordingly, you may not find the most recent issues here.

6.2   Council of Chief State School Officers (CCSSO)
www.ccsso.org
  CCSSO presents a rich and searchable site with extensive research information in many significant areas such as assessment, the arts, math and science, quality use of data, and leadership. The site includes a very convenient one-page link to all the state education departments in the U.S. and many reports and policy statements on key education issues. Readers will also find standards of knowledge, dispositions, and performance for new teachers and school administrators from the INTASC New Teacher Performance Assessment Project and the Interstate School Leaders Licensure Consortium.

6.3   Developing Educational Standards (DES)
edstandards.org/Standards.html

This is the best spot for direct information on standards from all the states, without question. It is organized by both state and subject. DES functions as a valuable national resource and was started by a local school district—the Putnam Valley Schools in New York. Now the site is cosponsored by the originator along with the Wappinger's Central School District, also in New York.

6.4   Education Commission of the States (ECS)
www.ecs.org

Find education policy for state leaders here. The site's links to "Federal Agencies," "Regional Education Labs," "National Organizations," and "Research Centers and Organizations" are particularly strong. ECS issued a document in early 2003 titled "The Roles and Responsibilities of School Boards and Superintendents" that is available online. A notable current initiative is *TQ Update*, the bimonthly newsletter of the ECS Teaching Quality Policy Center. Readers may receive this publication by e-mail subscription. ECS issues many research reports that are for sale.

6.5   Education Development Center (EDC)
www2.edc.org

In its "45-year history, EDC has evolved from a curriculum development laboratory specializing in science and mathematics to a global organization focused on learning and human development for people of all ages." This site creates access to all of EDC's current work and research, not just in education. Within the "School Improvement" area, readers may view all EDC projects organized into categories and connect to reports, articles, and resources that expand on each of them. Categories include "School Administration," "Global Projects," "Middle Grades," "Special Education and Inclusive Practices," "Equity and Diversity," "School Health," "Professional Development," "Curriculum," "Technology," "Community Partnerships," "School-to-Work," "Research and Evaluation," and "Higher Education."

6.6   *Education Next—A Journal of Opinion and Research*
www.educationnext.org

This generally conservative journal offers access to the current and all past issues. Its senior editor is Chester Finn, and the journal is published by the Hoover Institution at Stanford University.

6.7 *Education Policy Analysis Archives*
epaa.asu.edu/epaa

This is a peer-reviewed scholarly electronic journal of education policy. All articles are archived back to 1993, and the publication is fully searchable. *EPAA*'s reputation has grown steadily over the years.

6.8 Thomas B. Fordham Foundation
www.edexcellence.net

The Fordham Foundation provides a conservative view of educational policy and practice. The site is well organized and easy to navigate. It publishes numerous reports on areas of educational policy and also a weekly bulletin of news called the *Education Gadfly*, which is archived and fully indexed. The foundation has no connection with Fordham University.

6.9 MiddleWeb: Exploring Middle School Reform
www.middleweb.com

Would you like one-stop shopping for improving the education of young adolescents? MiddleWeb includes hundreds of original articles and links dealing with curriculum, teaching strategies, professional development, parent involvement, policy, and assessment. Of particular note are the weekly diaries written by an experienced teacher, a first-year teacher, a staff developer, and a principal. In addition, you can access four list-servs; subject area resources; a library of policy discussions; two free weekly e-newsletters; and "Of Particular Interest," containing many selected articles and resources for those devoted to middle school youth.

6.10 National Center for Education Statistics (NCES)
nces.ed.gov

How many students receive free lunch in the school district next door? How does the percentage of high school graduates compare between 1950 and now? How does the achievement of 15-year-old U.S. students compare to their counterparts in other countries? These questions are just the tip of the iceberg of what can be found at NCES. Good places to start on the home page are the Help section (which contains a very useful page on "Where Can I Find . . . ?") and the "Visit Popular NCES Sites" pull-down menu. In addition to online information, NCES publishes many reports and conducts conferences, training, and workshops on how to maximize use of its information.

6.11   National Center for Restructuring Education, Schools, and Teaching (NCREST)

www.tc.columbia.edu/ncrest

NCREST was founded by Linda Darling Hammond at Teachers College, Columbia University. It conducts and reports a great deal of important research studies, most of which are available from this site. General areas of interest to NCREST include "Restructuring," "Assessment," "Professional Development Schools," and "Cultural Interchange."

6.12   NCREL's Resource Center

www.ncrel.org/info/rc/index.html

The North Central Regional Educational Laboratory (NCREL) offers several research resources of great value. First, they will research an education topic for you and compile the information. Call 800-356-2735 or e-mail info@ncrel.org. You may also access a completed bibliography on any of 27 already researched topics. Approximately 15 to 20 percent of the citations are web based. Sample topics include: "Ability Grouping," "Charter Schools," "Closing the Achievement Gap," "Parent Involvement," "Teacher Quality," and "Technology and Student Achievement." These topics have also been assembled in Rapid Response Packets. NCREL will mail you a copy of the bibliography for a topic as well as several full-text copies of the most recent authoritative articles on the topic. Finally, through this site, readers may obtain a deep-discount subscription to the "Virtual Library" of the National Institute for Community Innovations. At only five dollars per person per year, this bargain subscription provides access to the H. W. Wilson Co.'s database of full-text articles from over 1,400 journals and magazines and access to the premium edition of *Encyclopedia Britannica*, among several other benefits. These discount subscriptions are available to educators as well as schools.

6.13   Open Access Journals in the Field of Education

aera-cr.asu.edu/ejournals

Readers will find links to more than 125 scholarly, peer-reviewed, full-text journals from around the world, available online at no cost.

6.14   Organization Links

www.edweek.org/context/orgs/org_alllisting.cfm

This is the largest and best organized listing of educational organizations on the net. More than 300 national organizations are given, with links to each of them as well as all state education departments. It is alphabetical and may also be searched by subject area.

6.15   Principal's Legislative Action Center—NASSP
capwiz.com/nassp/home

Here's a very useful and well-assembled site for those interested in political advocacy, media access, practical politics, and tracking election results. By typing in your zip code, you gain immediate access to all of your federal and state elected representatives, along with a report card on their voting records on key educational legislation as determined by the National Association of Secondary School Principals. An additional useful feature is access to major media outlets in your region for letters to the editor and general news releases. Direct e-mail is provided for most key editors, managers, and reporters in print and electronic media. While this site is intended for use by members of NASSP, it is accessible to anyone, and anyone can use the access it provides to contact elected representatives, lobby for desired policies and bills, and contact the mass media. A number of other organizations also use this valuable service provided by a company called Capitol Advantage.

6.16   RAND Institute on Education and Training
www.rand.org/education

Known most widely for its research on defense and security policy, RAND also performs very influential work in education. Many full-text reports are located here. Finding precisely what you want can be a challenge, but the quality of the material makes up for it.

6.17   Regional Educational Laboratory Network
www.relnetwork.org

This site is an exceptionally important resource for research. It provides a meta-search engine linking all 10 of the U.S. Regional Educational Laboratories (RELs) and their outstanding work. Each REL focuses on concerns related to its surrounding geographic area and also specializes in a designated topic area where it takes national leadership. Topics include "Assessment," "Reading and Language," "Educational

Leadership," "Expanded Learning Opportunities," "Family and Community Connections with Schools," "Re-Engineering Schools for Improvement," "Standards-Based Instructional Practice," "Teaching Diverse Learners," "Technology," and "Unlocking Today's Technology for Tomorrow's Students." Use of this search engine accesses all of the resources from all of the RELs.

6.18   Rethinking Schools Online
www.rethinkingschools.org

Rethinking Schools' flagship publication is the quarterly journal of the same name. The organization, composed mainly of activist teachers, is a nonprofit publisher of educational materials that advocates the reform of pre-K–12 education, with a strong emphasis on issues of equity and social justice. The current issue of the journal appears online, and issues are archived back to 1995. Back articles are indexed by title, and the site is searchable. Links are provided to a selection of other sites considered to be useful and important for educator-activists. Special resources have also been gathered for teaching about the war in Iraq.

6.19   School Redesign Network at Stanford University
www.schoolredesign.net

Linda Darling-Hammond serves as Principal Investigator of this group that focuses on small schools. The site offers research, tools, and resources to support those planning to implement small schools and others already doing the work. It includes videos, discussion boards, reports, and links to other organizations.

6.20   The Merrow Report
www.pbs.org/merrow/index.html

The Merrow Report appears on both public television and radio, providing documentary coverage of significant policy topics related to youth and learning. Four years of radio programs are accessible through the site as well as support materials for the television programs. Full-text transcripts of both radio and TV broadcasts are available, as well as references for further research. Videos of TV programs can be purchased. This is a good resource for quick and easy updates, particularly for laypeople.

6.21　United States Department of Education

www.ed.gov

This site is in a state of constant change as it reflects the ebb and flow of national policy in the crucial area of education. It contains a vast amount of fascinating information. The managers of the site work hard to make it as user-friendly as possible. You can even customize your use with a personal bookmark maker. Key information found here includes grants and contracts, financial aid, education resources ("PreK–12," "Higher Education," and "Career and Lifelong Learning"), research and statistics, policy statements, and news from the department. Most recent government reports on education can be downloaded for free, and links are provided to a wealth of resources for students, parents, teachers, principals, policy makers, and others. You can locate the name and phone number of all members of the Education Department staff and links to all of the federally supported research and assistance centers.

6.22　Wisconsin Center for Education Research (WCER)

www.wcer.wisc.edu

WCER is one of the foremost education research organizations in the nation. Its projects generally fall into the categories of special education, children, families, communities, policy, technology, English, higher education, mathematics, science, and professional development. Reports in each of these areas can be located under the area's name. The center's latest reports are contained in the *Working Papers Series*. Look for its online newsletters under "Online Publications."

Chapter Seven

Family Focus

7.1   Child and Family

www.nwrel.org/cfc

This program, from the Northwest Regional Educational Laboratory, hosts a number of initiatives: "School-Family-Community Partnerships" (described in item 2.10), "Language and Literacy Development," and "Early Connections" (dealing with technology in the education of preschool and primary age children). Each section contains a plentiful collection of online publications and links for further information. The Child and Family program also publishes an excellent e-newsletter. Each monthly issue contains a top-notch collection of links on important educational topics such as "Brain Development," "Homelessness," "Music," "Numeracy," and "Program Development."

7.2   Child and Family WebGuide

www.cfw.tufts.edu

Information displayed in this spot is selected by child-development specialists and organized into categories named "Family," "Education," "Health," "Typical Development," and "Childcare." A last category, "Activities" is organized by region and lists specific programs and things to do. Faculty at the Eliot-Pearson Department of Child Development at Tufts University created the site.

7.3   Connect for Kids (CFK)

www.connectforkids.org

CFK publishes two online magazines for adults concerned about kids. One e-zine is weekly, the other is monthly. The weekly tends to focus on news about kids and kid-related issues; the monthly is more feature oriented. The articles contain a great deal of information and guidance for adults, and, as a result, they are indexed for easy retrieval. Readers may search the site, or go the "Topics A-Z" index. Sample topics include "Adoption," "Arts," "Fathers," "Community Building," "Diversity and Awareness," and "Parenting."

7.4   National Parent Information Network (NPIN)
npin.org

NPIN's best feature is its "Virtual Library" of full-text articles, containing well over 1,000 quality-selected pieces of interest to parents and those who work with them. Also note the *Parent News* electronic magazine, published quarterly since 1995, that focuses on parenting and family involvement in education. All issues are archived here. In addition, NPIN offers a discussion board and a great list of print and online magazines and newsletters.

7.5   ParentSmart
www.parentsmart.com

Information to provide parents with the best, prescreened articles to help their children succeed in school is available in English, Spanish, and French. Readers may search ParentSmart's database of over 50,000 quality-selected articles or may start their research by reading reviews of articles in eight general topic areas. Educators who were instrumental in starting Upward Bound and Head Start organized the site.

7.6   Parent Soup
www.parentsoup.com

If you want to discuss parenting issues, this is the place to come. It contains hundreds of discussion groups and scheduled live chats. But do not miss the library, which houses thousands of articles that are browseable by topic and also searchable. Although much of the information can be helpful to dads as well as moms, ParentSoup is primarily aimed at the distaff side of the family.

7.7   PBS Kids
pbskids.org

From preschool to teens, PBS Kids has something for just about every young person. This home page is actually a portal to 37 different websites that PBS maintains for all of its broadcast shows as well as special online programs and services. There are games, stories, jokes, music, and coloring. Some pages even have streaming video and music. The site is really too large to try to describe in detail; users might begin by going to their favorite shows. Another way might be to surf some of the choices listed in the pull-down menu on the start page. All in all, this is a great place to have fun and learn for kids and families.

Chapter Eight

General Reference

8.1   Internet Public Library

www.ipl.org

Configured to occupy a place on the Internet similar to that occupied by a public library in a local community, IPL offers easy access to a highly organized collection of quality-selected websites. You can browse IPL similar to the way you might walk through the rows of shelves in a bricks and mortar library, ambling from topic to topic to see what might be interesting. Or, you can search using keywords or go into categories grouped under specific headings. The headings include "Subject Collections" such as "Arts & Humanities," "Education," and "Social Science"; "Ready Reference" containing "Almanacs," "Dictionaries," and "Biographies"; "Reading Room" housing online "Books," "Magazines," and "Newspapers"; "KidSpace"; "TeenSpace"; and "Special Collections." KidSpace and TeenSpace are particularly hospitable and useful for their intended audiences. Some highlights of IPL are that it's free and it has an online question and answer service ("Ask a Question"), POTUS ("Presidents of the United States" site for kids), term paper help (in TeenSpace), and the "Literary Criticism" collection in "Special Collections."

8.2   Journalist Express

www.journalistexpress.com

Just like you, reporters and writers need lots of information . . . fast. Hundreds of links are organized highly effectively to provide lightning-quick access to just the information you want. The "News" section connects to items such as magazines, broadcast news, gossip, and national and international newspapers. "Research and Resources" links to "Reference Sources," "Databases," "Photos," and "Investigation Sources." "People and Characters" links to "Phone and Email Locators," "Directories," "Experts," and "Discussion Communities." There's also a section of hotlinks for "Slow News Days." Some links go to sites that may require registration or subscription.

8.3   Librarians Index to the Internet (LII)
lii.org

Hosted by UC Berkeley SunSITE and sponsored by the Library of California, LII is organized as an annotated subject directory of more than 11,000 Internet resources. Sources are carefully selected by librarians for their reliability and trustworthiness and are intended for use by the general public and librarians. Readers may sign up for *New This Week*, a weekly e-mail newsletter that contains the most recent additions to the collection. The site is organized into 14 major categories and operates a robust search engine.

8.4   Refdesk
www.refdesk.com

Make this your first stop for reference information. In addition to encyclopedias and online news services, Refdesk links to many national and international newspapers, calculators, weather, quotations, urban legends, facts on file, and lots, lots more. Refdesk is searchable and very user-friendly. Do not miss the "Ask Bob" section (listed under "Site Information") where a live person responds to your research questions—a great place to go when you just want to surf.

8.5   StartSpot Network
www.startspot.com/network

Here is a home page that connects to tons of top quality-selected spots. Each spot specializes in a particular topic area and provides essential as well as fun information. There are 13 spots: "BookSpot," "CinemaSpot," "EmploymentSpot," "GenealogySpot," "GiveSpot," "GourmetSpot," "GovSpot," "HeadlineSpot," "HomeworkSpot," "LibrarySpot," "MuseumSpot," "PeopleSpot," and "TripSpot."

Chapter Nine

Grants

9.1   Guide Star
www.guidestar.org

Guide Star gives access to the tax returns of every nonprofit organization in the country required to report to the IRS; invaluable information for grant seekers. It also publishes a free e-zine on philanthropy and grants. Registration is required, but free.

9.2   SchoolGrants
www.schoolgrants.org

For the first-time seeker or seasoned veteran, SchoolGrants can be extremely helpful. It lists grant opportunities at the federal and state levels, provides grant-writing tips, gives samples of successful proposals, suggests numerous ways to do fundraising in addition to or instead of grants, publishes a free e-newsletter, and hosts a listserv and discussion forum for those who wish to discuss their work.

9.3   SRA International GrantsWeb
www.srainternational.org/newweb/grantsweb/index.cfm

Here is the best single grants site on the web. It contains both government and private grants information for all parts of the U.S. government was well as Canada, Australia, Great Britain, and Israel. The primary focus of GrantsWeb is university researchers, but K–12 people will also find it without peer. It also contains extensive policy information, regulations, and sources of information of interest to the grants professional.

9.4   The Foundation Center
www.fdncenter.org

The world of private grants can be quite a challenge to navigate. You can find excellent help here with the "User-Friendly Guide," "Proposal Writing Short Course," and "Electronic Reference Desk." You may also subscribe to the e-mail *Philanthropy News Digest* that publishes short pieces on the field every week. It is archived back to 1995 and fully searchable. "PND Job Corner" is a great source of job information in the philanthropic and nonprofit arenas.

9.5   TRAM Research Funding Opportunities and Administration
tram.east.asu.edu

TRAM functions as another outstanding source of grant-related information. The section on sources of grant funds is updated daily. The "Research Funding Opportunities" section enables you to find specific U.S. government programs through a search engine limited to its pages. TRAM is well-known for its great online collection of forms from many agencies and also provides links to the sponsored research offices of over 225 American colleges and universities. The purpose of these sites is to make it easy to find and apply for grants—use them!

Chapter Ten

Homework Help

10.1   B. J. Pinchbeck's Homework Helper
school.discovery.com/homeworkhelp/bjpinchbeck/
This site is an elegant piece of work started by a father and his son when the younger one was in elementary school. It is organized by subjects and then subcategories underneath and provides links to other sites with some guiding commentary. B. J.'s spot is agreeably organized.

10.2   Cyber Study Hall: A Guide to Homework Help Online
www.education-world.com/a_tech/tech061.shtml
This article describes 40 sites for homework help, including general sites, subject-specific ones, and sites created by kids.

10.3   FactMonster
factmonster.com/homework
An atlas, dictionary, almanac, encyclopedia, and homework help all rolled into one. FactMonster is full of facts and interesting information, as well as games, quizzes, and changing daily features such as today's birthday, today in history, and word of the day. FactMonster looks like it is for grade school kids, but everyone—including adults—can learn a lot here. Homework Center covers the standard school subjects and also offers assistance in topics such as writing, taking notes, studying for tests, giving an oral report, and conducting an interview.

10.4   HomeworkSpot
www.homeworkspot.com

This is practically an encyclopedia, with its links to information all over the web. The site is generally organized by subject links down the left side, organized by "Elementary," "Middle," and "High School." Each school level ends with a "Study Break," where games and fun activities are located. Also check the "Reference Desk," which connects to "Ask an Expert" sites, "Biographies," "Calculators," "Lists," "Quotations," and "Statistics."

10.5   Hotmath
www.hotmath.org

Hotmath has free tutorial solutions to odd-numbered homework problems in the most common secondary textbooks used in prealgebra, algebra, precalculus, calculus, and geometry. After clicking on the appropriate textbook and page number, a student is guided through an interactive tutorial consisting of explained hints and steps, leading to the solution. Hotmath uses the language of the particular textbook in guiding students.

10.6   KidsClick!
sunsite.berkeley.edu/kidsclick!

This is a nice, comprehensive search site for kids, organized by librarians. Topics lead to websites selected by library specialists for accuracy, reliability, and suitability for kids in grades K–7. The start page consists of fifteen general categories such as "Facts & Reference," "Science & Math," "Health & Family," and "Geography/History/Biography." Each general category is subdivided into specific subjects. More than 600 specific subjects are catalogued; they can be searched by general category, first letter, or keyword. KidsClick! presents a couple of really neat and distinctive features: (1) by clicking on "Librarian's Eyes" at the bottom of the start page, the page is transformed into a Dewey Decimal catalog; (2) by clicking on "Picture Search Tools" or "Sound Search Tools" at the top of the start page, the reader is taken to hotlinks for preselected search engines specializing in images or sounds that are free, legal, and kid-friendly.

10.7   Multnomah County Library Homework Center
www.multnomah.lib.or.us/lib/homework/index.html

MHC was organized, and I do mean organized, by librarians for middle and high school students in their community and is now available to everyone. Topical subject headings lead to annotated links. The "Social Issues" collection is particularly well done.

10.8   Sparknotes

www.sparknotes.com

Produced by Barnes & Noble, Sparknotes offers more than 1,000 free, online study guides. Although originally published for "Literature," "Drama," "Shakespeare," "Philosophy," and "Poetry," the guides now also include "Math," "Chemistry," "Economics," "Computer Science," "History," "Physics," "Psychology," "Health & Nutrition," "Biography," "Biology," and "Astronomy." In addition, Sparknotes also offers inexpensive online SAT and ACT test preparation.

Chapter Eleven

Law and Finance

11.1   Brigham Young University Education and Law Journal
www.law2.byu.edu/jel

Education and Law Journal (ELJ) is published twice a year, featuring articles on educational and legal issues affecting elementary, secondary, and higher education. Back issues are archived here.

11.2   Education Finance (EDFIN) Home Page
nces.ed.gov/edfin

Graphics on comparative education spending are fascinating, and the "Peer Search" tool permits one to compare a district's spending to others similar to it. Many publications are available online. One I find particularly noteworthy is *Characteristics of the 100 Largest Public Elementary and Secondary School Districts in the United States,* which is published annually. Nearly 25 percent of America's students are enrolled in these 100 districts.

11.3   Education Law
www.megalaw.com/top/education.php

This is a great location for the deep student of education law. It contains links to recent U.S. Supreme Court and Appellate Court education law decisions, federal education statutes and regulations, education statutes for every state, the six major federal government education agencies, every state education department website, and more than 25 other sites dealing with education law.

11.4   Education Week–School Finance
www.edweek.org/context/topics/issuespage.cfm?id=22

In a brief article, *Education Week* gives a rapid overview of some of the considerations involved in school finance. Links are provided to recent articles in the publication, online resources consulted in writing the article, and resources for further investigation.

11.5   Legal Lowdown
www.nassp.org/service/legal_lowdown.cfm

Here is an archive of informative and practical articles on legal matters as they affect school administrators, from the National Association of Secondary School Principals. This URL takes you to the most recent article. Scroll down to the bottom of the page to access the complete archive of legal articles, going back to June 2001.

11.6   National Center on Education Finance (NCEF)
www.ncsl.org/programs/educ/NCEF.htm

This organization was created in 2000 by the National Conference of State Legislatures "to help legislators, legislative staff, and other policy-makers wrestle with the complex issues in education finance." Accordingly, information on the site comes from a state perspective. NCEF publishes an annual review of education finance litigation and maintains a 50-state education finance formula database. Additional publications include *State Efforts to Define Adequacy in Education Finance*, *Special Education Finance*, and *Fiscal Implications of NCLB*. Their online *Monthly Memo* tracks finance developments at the federal level and in all states and also highlights significant online reports issued each month by other organizations. NCEF maintains a collection of links to research reports on topics including "Adequacy and Equity," "Class Size," "Education Finance Formulas," "Cost Adjustments and Indexes," "Property Taxes," "Special Education," and "School Facilities."

11.7   School Finance—Consortium for Policy Research in Education (CPRE)
www.wcer.wisc.edu/cpre/finance

The CPRE School Finance Project conducts research and disseminates information on this topic. Research focuses on "Expenditures for Instructional Improvement," "Resource Allocation," "School-Based Budgeting," and "Program Adequacy." Two unique features found here are the "School

Redesign Report" and case studies. The "Report" enables a school to decide whether it can afford to restructure using one of several comprehensive school reform designs. The case studies (found in the Links section) provide rich descriptions of elementary and secondary schools' efforts to restructure through resource allocation, professional development, and/or school-based budgeting.

11.8   School Law Issues

www.nsba.org/site/page_cosa.asp?TRACKID=&CID=381&DID=8622

Quick links to information provided by the Council of School Attorneys, affiliated with the National School Boards Association. Topics addressed include "Athletics," "Curriculum," "Employment," "Equity and Discrimination," "Finance," "Health," "Legal System," "Liability," "Local Governance," "Property and Facilities," "No Child Left Behind," "Religion," "School Reform," "School Safety," "Student Achievement," "Student Rights," and "Technology." Each topic includes targeted information including resources, news, and recent cases.

Chapter Twelve

(Mostly) Lesson Plans

12.1   A to Z Lesson Plans

www.atozteacherstuff.com/lessonplans

More than 300 teacher-created lessons can be found here, searchable by grade level or subject. Most material is at the elementary level. A to Z also hosts 13 chat rooms, provides feature articles, and offers numerous printables. In addition, this site links to LessonPlanz.com, where one can locate more than 2,000 lesson plans.

12.2   Awesome Library

www.awesomelibrary.org

The Awesome Library is aptly named. It takes more than 22,000 links and organizes them for teachers, kids, teens, parents, librarians, and college students so that desired information is quick and easy to find. One can browse the site in 14 languages in addition to English. Thousands of lesson plans are offered at all levels and in all subject areas. Be sure to investigate the Awesome Talking Library, where the computer can "read" aloud to students or to you from online articles, pages, or books. Students can read along to text, and you can listen to an article while driving or doing something around your workplace or home. Awesome.

12.3   Best Practices of Technology Integration

www.remc11.k12.mi.us/bstpract

Find over 1,000 lesson plans here, intended to integrate technology into standards-based teaching and learning. The plans have been created by Michigan teachers and tested in the classroom prior to posting. They are organized by subject and grade level.

12.4   Blue Web'n Applications Library

www.kn.sbc.com/wired/bluewebn

Every week, Blue Web'n adds to its total of over 1,800 quality-selected activities, projects, tools, lessons, hotlists, and other resources in the "Arts," "Business," "Community Interest," "Education," "English," "Foreign Language," "Health and Physical Education," "History and Social Studies," "Mathematics," "Science," "Technology," and "Vocational Education." Navigation through Blue Web'n ("blue ribbon" + "web") is easy, and each entry is both described and given a rating. You may register to receive a new list of five chosen sites in your e-mail every week, browse the main site, or search it by grade level, broad subject level, or specific subcategory.

12.5   Educator's Reference Desk

www.eduref.org

ERD takes over where askERIC left off. It is operated by essentially the same people but with a different source of financial support. Readers may find here the lesson plan bank of more than 2,000 lessons formerly located at ERIC, along with more than 3,000 links to education information and over 200 archived responses to reader questions.

12.6   eThemes

emints.more.net/ethemes

These folks from Missouri have a great idea. They have identified over 500 thematic subjects and combed the net for the best resources to use in teaching the particular themes. For example, go to "Aviation: Wright Brothers" and immediately locate 18 sites with written information, photos, an audio interview, and even a film clip. Themes are related to the state's performance and knowledge standards.

12.7   Gateway to Educational Materials (GEM)

www.thegateway.org

Here is an elegantly simple way to search over 27,000 education resources, mostly lesson plans and websites. Resources may be free or not. The search template is nicely assembled for ease of use and clarity of search. The collection may also be browsed. GEM is supported by many outstanding contributing organizations and is updated often. All materials are quality reviewed according to established criteria.

12.8   IDEAS
ideas.wisconsin.edu

Teachers in Wisconsin have worked in teams to select websites from all across the web, evaluate them, describe them, and connect them to state standards. The site consists of lesson plans, teaching resources, professional development opportunities, and spots for students. IDEAS is searchable by grade level, subject, or keyword. It also contains 95 short movies in the section called "VideoIDEAS."

12.9   Lesson Plans Library from DiscoverySchool.com
school.discovery.com/lessonplans/index.html

Hundreds of teacher-developed lesson plans, searchable by grade level and subject, from the Discovery Channel.

12.10   Lesson Plans on the Web
www.ncela.gwu.edu/classroom/lessons.htm

This site is plain and simple, and very useful. It focuses on sites that collect high-quality lesson plans. It has a particularly strong collection of sites for bilingual and ESL, and each of the 28 selected lesson-plan sources is described briefly.

12.11   New York Times Learning Network (free, but registration required)
www.nytimes.com/learning

There are sections of this site for students, teachers, and parents. Teachers can access a daily lesson plan for grades 6–12 (developed in cooperation with Bank Street College); all are archived and also grouped into thematic units. Students can read the day's top news stories, take a news quiz, and play special crossword puzzles. They can also submit letters to the editor and ask a reporter a question. Additionally, vocabulary and test-taking exercises are given. The "News Snapshot" section is aimed at students in grades 3–5 and provides a daily photo and questions dealing with its related news story. These appear five days a week and are archived back to 1999. Parents can discuss current events with their children using "Conversation Starters," join in an online discussion, and explore the family movie guide.

12.12   PBS TeacherSource
www.pbs.org/teachersource/index.htm

This is a great spot for teachers, offering over 4,000 lesson plans and activities that are searchable by subject area and by match to state, U.S. national, and Canadian national standards. The "Technology and Teaching" section gives tutorials, ideas for integrating technology across the curriculum, research, and in-depth online professional development. PBS TV listings for the current month and the next month are located here, and PBS publishes a weekly e-mail newsletter specifically for teachers containing new web features, details on upcoming programs with taping rights, station resources, professional development opportunities, and products from PBS Video.

12.13   TeacherVision.com Lesson Planning Center
www.teachervision.com/lesson-plans/lesson-5775.html?detoured=1

More than 5,000 lesson plans, resources, and activities are located here. Browse through the lessons and also review the dozens of printable worksheets and graphic organizers, scores of cross-curricular themes, assessment resources (including an online gradebook), reference sources for teachers and students, and online student activities.

12.14   The Solution Site
www.thesolutionsite.com

This site has been created by the state of West Virginia to feature lessons that deeply involve students in their own education. At the same time, the units integrate technology, curriculum, teaching, learning, and evaluation. It will eventually grow to over 1,000 lessons/units, all developed by teacher teams. Each lesson or unit is keyed to both state and national learning standards. TSS is quite user friendly and searchable by subject, state standard, grade level, keyword, or by multiple items.

Chapter Thirteen

Museums

13.1   The Artist's Toolkit
www.artsconnected.org/toolkit
The Walker Art Center and Minneapolis Institute of Arts have created an outstanding hands-on tool to explore the elements and principals used to create works of art. These topics include "Line," "Color," "Space," "Shape," "Balance," and "Movement/Rhythm." Each topic includes animated demonstrations, examples from works of art, and opportunities to create your own composition. I love the creative part. Educators are encouraged to visit the "For Your Classroom" section at www.artsconnected .org/classroom. It contains learning activities, lesson plans, links, and a downloadable *Teacher's Guide to ArtsConnectEd*.

13.2   Art Tales: Telling Stories with Wildlife Art
www.wildlifeart.org/ArtTales/index.html
This wonderful, award-winning site from the National Museum of Wildlife Art in Jackson Hole, Wyoming, offers opportunities for skill development in observation, imagination, multimedia presentation, and writing. Students choose to be a frontier explorer, field guide writer, or museum curator, each role having its own task to perform. They are asked to select artworks from the museum's collection and either create a story, write a wildlife field guide, or create a museum exhibit—all online. They may add music and sound effects and then publish their work on the museum's website.

13.3   Campfire Stories with George Catlin
catlinclassroom.si.edu

George Catlin was an artist, ethnologist, and showman who traveled through the Great Plains to document Native American culture in the 1830s. He visited more than 140 tribes, producing more than 500 artworks and extensive writing. This extraordinarily rich multimedia site is organized around four core themes: "Indian Removal from Ancestral Lands," "Choices and Consequences of Catlin's Quest," "Leadership Qualities of Chiefs and Others," and "Ecology Systems of the Western Landscape." The core themes are each enlivened through recorded interviews of contemporary sources (the "Campfire Stories"), a gallery of artworks and exhibition labels, a timeline, and maps. Written interview transcripts are also provided. Extensive lesson plans are included that address standards in middle and high school history, geography, art appreciation, environmental conservation, and multicultural studies; however, the site is also designed so that educators may plan for themselves how to use it best with their students. Produced by the Smithsonian American Art Museum.

13.4   Exploratorium
www.exploratorium.edu
Museums educate, and this is one of the best. Exploratorium bills itself as "the museum of science, arts, and human perception." The website offers online activities, more than 25 online exhibitions, scores of excellent current and archived webcasts on fascinating topics going back to 1996 (!), hands-on activities, science news, a terrific e-zine that includes multimedia and hands-on activities, an educators' newsletter, and much more. Winner of many awards.

13.5   Fine Arts Museums of San Francisco
www.thinker.org
These two fine museums (The Legion of Honor and the de Young Museum) have combined their resources to create "The Thinker Image Base," consisting of over 82,000 searchable images. The online "Virtual Gallery" enables users to select images and arrange them in their own online exhibition.

13.6   Kids Design Network
www.dupagechildrensmuseum.org/kdn
Elementary students respond to engineering challenges by designing a gadget to solve a particular problem such as building an alarm for their

bedroom door. Students may draw their design online and chat in real time with an engineer, who gives feedback on the student proposal. Students then build their gadgets, in groups, with recycled materials. A carefully prepared "Teacher's Guide" supports the process every step of the way. KDN is supported by the DuPage Children's Museum, Naperville, Illinois.

13. 7   Museums and the Web: Best of the Web
www.archimuse.com/mw2003/best/index.html
www.archimuse.com/mw2002/best/index.html
www.archimuse.com/mw2001/best/index.html
www.archimuse.com/mw2000/best/index.html
www.archimuse.com/mw99/best/index.html
www.archimuse.com/mw98/best/index.html
www.archimuse.com/mw97/mw97best.htm#best

Archives and Museum Informatics has made awards for the best museum sites on the web since 1997. Award categories have changed over the years and currently include "Best Online Exhibition," "Best E-Services," "Best Educational Use," "Best Innovative or Experimental Application," "Best Museum Professional's Site," "Best Museum Research Site," and "Best Overall Museum Site." Do not just focus on the winners; nearly all the entries have a great deal to offer. Readers will find outstanding creative work and extremely imaginative ways to use the web for enjoyment and learning. It would be nice if the designers of this site made finding the various museum sites a bit more user-friendly.

13.8   Museum Sites Online from the Museum Computer Network
www.mcn.edu/resources/sitesonline.htm

Look here to find an alphabetical list giving links to over 1,700 U.S. and international museum and museum-related websites.

13.9   Online Workshop: Teaching about the Holocaust
www.ushmm.org/education/foreducators/guidelines

This online workshop, produced by the United States Holocaust Memorial Museum, provides a complete and well-organized workshop on teaching about the Holocaust. It includes lesson plans, suggested topics, and extensive multimedia resources. Video interviews with survivors as well as an exhaustive, downloadable *Resource Book* constitute excellent features, along with numerous photographs and other primary sources.

13.10   Resources for Learning
www.amnh.org/education/resources

Enter this portal to the American Museum of Natural History to locate all of its online resources for the public. Readers may browse by
general topics such as anthropology, astronomy, biology, earth science,
and paleontology—or look through special thematic collections, from
the famed Ology site for 7- to 12-year-olds (winner of acclaimed
awards all by itself) to "Einstein" and the "Hall of Biodiversity." Abundant lesson plans and guides for families may be found everywhere. Do
not miss the guide for first-time users, it is a big help.

13.11   Theban Mapping Project
www.thebanmappingproject.com

This is an astonishing compilation of resources dealing with Thebes.
The project, based at the American University in Cairo, has compiled a
dazzling array of photographs, articles, maps, 65 narrated tours, a 3-D
recreation of tomb KV 14, and a fabulous aerial atlas photograph of the
Theban Necropolis, which allows viewers to zoom in and out to see details of temples and palaces. This is for true enthusiasts of Egyptology;
guides for teachers are not provided.

13.12   Top Ten Online Art Museums for Kids
www.kidsart.com/topten

Somehow we have this love-hate relationship with top-ten lists. They
make life easier for those who refer to them, but they create a winners-
and-losers mentality that makes it seem if you are not on this list you are
not any good, which we all know to be untrue. Having gotten that guilt off
our chest, this is a neat little web page. Not only does it provide links to
the museum sites mentioned in its title, but it gives eight more fun top-ten
lists related to art education for young people: "Top Ten Things to Use for
a Monster Costume," "Top Ten Periods in Western Art History," "Top Ten
Music for Abstract Art," "Top Ten Things to Remember When You Teach
Art," "Top Ten Coupons for Kids to Give Their Parents," "Top Ten Unusual Color Names to Learn," "Top Ten Collage Collections," and "Top
Ten Favorite American Artists for Kids to Know."

Chapter Fourteen

Personal Productivity

14.1 Biopoint

www.biopoint.com/webtools/webtools.html

Click on "Personal Productivity Web Tools" to find a comprehensive suite of tools, file storage, bookmark management, network security, file conversion to PDF or HTML, clip art, online survey wizards, fax receiving, web-searching tools, web-page production, and web-page hosting—all free! Go to "Course Productivity Web Tools" for more than a dozen free sites that help educators create inquiry-based online learning documents, rubrics, and online quizzes; save web pages for offline viewing; create online discussion groups; and construct bibliographies easily.

14.2 Citysearch

www.citysearch.com

Taking a long trip, or just going into the city? Use Citysearch to find out about entertainment, shopping, hotels, nightlife, restaurants, events, and businesses. Nearly every big city in every state is included along with 35 international destinations.

14.3 doneasy

www.doneasy.com/index.php

E-mail (including forwarding from other accounts), calendaring (with e-mail reminders), message boards, private and public chat rooms, online address book, online bookmarks (store all your passwords), online diary/journal, and 10 MB of storage—all free and all in the same place.

14.4   Daily Dose of the Web

www.internet4classrooms.com/daily_dose.htm

This clever site gives you multitudes of new things every day to do with students. It contains links to question of the day sites, subject matter sites, quotations sites, brain teasers, and interesting trivia. Each category contains multiple sites that change their content every day. Use these for discussion starters, sponge activities, extensions for fast workers, or any other time you need something quick, interesting, and fun.

14.5   Do It Yourself Home Improvement, Repair, Remodeling, and Hardware Store

doityourself.com

Let's face it, we all need this information sometime. Not only does this site give specific instructions for "Home Improvement and Repair," "Automotive," "Decorating and Crafts," "Gardening and Landscaping," and "Lifestyle and Finance"—but if you have something that takes more time or expertise than you can muster, DoItYourself.com also lists prescreened, qualified contractors. Lots of hardware products and how-to guides are also on sale. The "Interactive How-to Workshop" even offers animated demonstration videos with sound. Picked as a top site by both *Time* magazine and *PC Magazine* in 2003.

14.6   epicurious

eat.epicurious.com

This may be the web's best site on food, providing more than 16,000 recipes. But it is chock full of lots more than that. Slide shows display great dishes with instant links to recipes for their preparation. Videos demonstrate food preparation. Wine guides and drink-mixing how-to's are provided along with restaurant guides to more than 50 U.S. and world destinations. Excerpts appear from *Bon Appetit* and *Gourmet* magazines, more than a dozen forums are hosted, and travel tips and deals are also provided.

14.7   Free Email Reminder Service

www.candor.com/reminder/default.asp

Automatically receive an e-mail reminder for any date you specify. Reminders can be set to come one day, three days, one week, or two weeks before the specified date. Your reminder message can be up to 250 characters. Never forget an important personal date or deadline again. Send reminders to yourself to keep long-term projects on schedule.

14.8   iKeepBookmarks.com—A Web-Based Bookmark Manager
www.ikeepbookmarks.com

Do you regularly use more than one computer? Use both Explorer and Netscape? Do you ever want to share your favorite pages with colleagues or friends? This free site enables you to easily upload and keep your bookmarks online. You can create separate profiles for individuals, have only one set of bookmarks for home and work, and not have to worry about moving your favorites when you get a new computer. You can even make them public for others to access, or keep them private for your own use. I used iKeepBookmarks to do the research for this book. It simplified my work tremendously.

There is another similar site called Backflip (at www.backflip.com), but I prefer iKeepBookmarks. I find its interface easier to use, and published reports have questioned Backflip's financial health.

14.9   Medical Information
MayoClinic.com: www.mayoclinic.com
MEDLINEplus: www.medlineplus.gov
WebMDHealth: my.webmd.com/webmd_today/home/default

Check your symptoms or your medication; ask an expert or subscribe to a newsletter; read medical news or take a brief health course; shop for health insurance or research a disease; consult a medical encyclopedia or search for clinical trials; find a doctor or dentist; or read up on wellness. These are the three top-rated sites for medical consumers.

14.10   My ParenTime's Printable Checklists
www.printablechecklists.com

What a great idea! Checklists to help us remember all the details we struggle with and to build good habits in young people. These are designed primarily for families. Use them as handouts for parent meetings, workshops, newsletters, and whatever else you can think of. Educators will probably find the sections of the site titled "Home & Household," "Children/Education," and "Parenting" to be the most useful.

14.11   My Teacher Tools: Rona's Ultimate Flashcard Tools for Teachers
www.myteachertools.com/flashcards.php

The needs served by flash cards will probably never disappear from schools. Here is one place to go for just about all the flash cards you will ever need.

14.12   Ofoto
www.ofoto.com/Welcome.jsp

Ofoto is consistently rated the best picture site on the web, so good that Kodak bought it. Create photo albums online and send them to anyone you want—a great way to share the wonderful things going on in your school with families and community members.

14.13   Teacher Time Savers
www.learnnc.org/index.nsf/doc/timesavers?OpenDocument

Just about every month, Bobby Hopgood from North Carolina writes a quick article on how to use free web tools for education. They are consistently practical, well written, and very creative. This site hosts them all; keep checking back for the newest edition. Examples include "Concept Maps," "Creating Free Calendars Online," "Creating Online Surveys," and "Make It Visible: Create a Graph!".

14.14   The Motley Fool
www.fool.com

Quite simply the web's busiest and favorite site for personal financial management.

14.15   www.4teachers | Tools
www.4teachers.org/4teachers/tools/index.shtml

The High Plains Regional Technology in Education Center has created 10 outstanding online tools to help teachers save time and integrate technology in their teaching. "Notable Pics" enables the addition of written notes to areas of a photo. "Assign-A-Day" creates a student calendar for each class or subject. "Casa Notes" facilitates creation of customizable, typical notes to send home in English and Spanish. "Think Tank" helps 3rd to 8th graders refine their research topics so they become more manageable for Internet searching. NoteStar enables teachers to assign and keep track of group projects and helps students manage research, take notes from the web, and create printable notes and a bibliography.

RubiStar helps teachers easily create and store rubrics in virtually all subjects. RubiStar can also be used to analyze task performance by the class as a whole. It is available in English, Spanish, and Dutch. Quiz Star enables creation of custom online quizzes. TrackStar permits the creation of annotated online lessons to guide students through teacher-chosen sites. Quizzes can be built in. "Project Based Learning Checklists" make possible easy teacher creation of student-performance checklists for multimedia projects, written reports, oral presentations, and science projects. "Web Worksheet Wizard" makes creation of a worksheet, lesson, or web page quick and easy.

14.16 Yahoo Services
Address Book: login.yahoo.com/config/login?.src=ab&z=1&.intl=us& .done=http%3a//address.yahoo.com/yab/us%3f.rand=24980138%26v=SA
Briefcase: briefcase.yahoo.com
Calendar: login.yahoo.com/config/login_verify2?.src=yc&.intl=&.partner=& .done=http%3a//calendar.yahoo.com/?
Driving Directions: maps.yahoo.com/py/ddResults.py?Pyt=Tmap

"Address Book" and "Calendar" enable users to keep their information online so it may be accessed from any computer with an Internet connection. "Briefcase" provides 30 MB of free file storage. With "Driving Directions," enter the address you want to drive from and the one you want to get to. You will receive turn-by-turn instructions for every step of the way, along with a map of the full route and another of the area around your destination. While Yahoo's driving directions are the most popular, many (including *Time* magazine) think that a similar service provided by Rand McNally is better. It can be found at www.randmcnally.com.

Chapter Fifteen

Preparing for College and Career

15.1   Career Key: Choosing a Career

www.careerkey.org

Career Key is a free, online career assessment instrument; it measures a person's skills, abilities, values, interests, and personality. After taking the assessment, a participant receives a profile on career and college choices, or changing a career, or career planning advice. Career Key is intended for both students and career changers and is available in both English and Chinese.

15.2   Career Voyages

www.careervoyages.gov

The U.S. Departments of Labor and Education have joined together to produce Career Voyages. The site offers career guidance for those over 18 who may possess education and training at all levels, from a high school diploma to a graduate degree—including technical and on-the-job training and work experience. Extensive information is offered on job and career opportunities and areas of growth, organized nationally and by state. In addition, readers can focus on opportunities for youth, career changers, parents, or career advisors. Readers can locate general pay information and training requirements. The "Tools" section gives links to a great deal more information, much of it quite specific and helpful. Do check the "Video Voyage" area that includes videos of real workers in jobs that require apprentice training, on-the-job training, two-year college degrees, or no degrees.

15.3   CollegeNET

www.collegenet.com

CollegeNET has three distinctive strengths: an extensive online scholarship search capability (free), the CollegeBOT search engine that looks for user-entered keywords on all college sites (free), and the StandOut service to create an online profile to encourage colleges to recruit you (fee based). In addition to a college search service, CollegeNET also facilitates electronic applications to more than 1,500 colleges.

15.4   FastWeb
www.fastweb.com

This site contains the largest free online database for scholarships, grants, and fellowships—consisting of over 600,000 scholarships worth over $1 billion. In addition, FastWeb provides expert tips on financial aid and careers, a personalized matching tool for college selection, and a fee-based service to assist students in being recruited by their college of choice. Be advised that FastWeb sells the student information it collects to other parties.

15.5   O*NET Career Exploration Tools
www.onetcenter.org/tools.html

The federal government has replaced the *Dictionary of Occupational Titles* with this website known as the Occupational Information Network, or O*NET. O*NET exists to serve as "the nation's primary source of occupational information." The overall site houses a remarkable array of resources and information. The "Career Exploration Tools" serve as one fascinating aspect. Readers will find here five separate online assessment instruments to "identify . . . work-related interests, what they consider important on the job, and . . . abilities." Some of the instruments can be self-administered online, others require third-party administration. All necessary material is available for free online or for purchase in hard copy.

15.6   Peterson's Education Portal
www.petersons.com

Long known as one of the key providers of information to students, parents, and educators about college education, Peterson's has created a site that offers great resources and help for free, as well as other services for a fee. Included are descriptions of K–12 private schools, undergraduate and graduate colleges and universities, study abroad, summer programs, corporate training, career education, resume services, distance learning, college applications to download, information on financing college education, college search, ordering information for Peterson's products, and much more. A key feature of this site is its EssayEdge editing service for undergraduate, graduate, and professional school admission essays. While this service is fee based, it offers an extensive amount of free help too.

15.7   The College Board
www.collegeboard.com

Extensive guidance in "Planning for College," "Taking the Tests," "Finding the Right College," "Getting into College," and "Paying for College" for students, parents, and education professionals can be found in this location. Of course, you can register for the SAT and related tests and also purchase moderately priced study materials. A great feature is "My Organizer" (fee based) that gives additional online help in test preparation, a fee-based guidance service for careers and college majors, early receipt and transmission of test scores (fee based), online admissions and scholarship applications, and more.

15.8   *U.S. News and World Report*—America's Best Colleges and Graduate Schools
www.usnews.com/usnews/edu/eduhome.htm

Online, browseable versions of *U.S. News*'s well-known guides to "America's Best Colleges," "America's Best Graduate Schools," and "E-learning" are found in this location. Free versions may be upgraded to more robust information for a fee, and of course, the hard-copy versions may be purchased. Other features include an extensive five-step guide to "conquer college admissions" and considerable advice on paying for college.

Chapter Sixteen

Professional Development

16.1   Active Learning with Technology (ALT)
www.southcentralrtec.org/alt/alt.html

ALT is a complete professional development package for groups of teachers. The program's goal "is to assist teachers in developing and implementing learner-centered environments supported by technology." Instructional modules develop teachers' skills in integrating technology through use of inquiry-based, project-based, and small group learning. All necessary instructional materials, including handouts, instructions for facilitators, and video clips for viewing and discussion are provided online.

The first 6 of the 16 instructional modules are designed to be presented in a sequence of two full days. The remaining 10 modules comprise approximately 42 hours of instructional time and may be presented in any order, according to your schedule. The package was developed by the South Central Regional Technology Education Center and field tested with 350 teachers.

16.2   ALPS (Active Learning Practices in Schools)
learnweb.harvard.edu/alps/home/index.cfm

Project Zero, at Harvard's Graduate School of Education, built ALPS to operate as an online collaborative environment to improve instruction and educational practice through active engagement of students in their own learning. ALPS consists of three regions: "The Thinking Classroom," "Teaching for Understanding," and "Education with New Technologies." Each region provides instructional tools and resources; model lessons, projects, and activities; interactive conferences and online workshops; online and downloadable curriculum design tools; and interactive forums for teacher project collaboration. Within ALPS, educators can learn about a number of specific approaches to cultivate student understanding; download articles and resources; design curriculum online; collaborate with other teachers; create a personal portfolio of projects and lessons; publish one's own materials and tools; give and receive feedback on ideas, lessons, and activities; and create interdisciplinary projects across subjects and/or grade levels.

16.3 Brain Connection
www.brainconnection.com

Brain Connection is a comprehensive resource on brain research and its educational applications. The section titled "Education Connection" presents a series of articles that relate brain science to teaching and learning. "Brain Basics" provides animations, images, online courses, student activities and experiments, and facts to help adults and young people learn about the brain. The "Talk" section includes columns, interviews, and detailed summaries of conference presentations by leading authorities on the brain and education. Games, illusions, and brain teasers show both the strengths and limitations of our brains. Books and websites are also reviewed.

16.4 By Your Own Design (BYOD)
www.enc.org/professional/guide

This is a fascinating model for using technology to support educators in the preparation, implementation, and assessment of their own personal plan for professional development—centered mainly on mathematics and science. After reading a few introductory articles, participants are led to an area where they develop a personal plan using the forms and templates provided. Then they analyze the factors that may contribute to, or inhibit, their efforts toward success. Next, participants are offered a wealth of specific learning strategies and, finally, a plan for assessing progress. Several areas of BYOD contain video and audio clips that supplement the content on the page, and extensive additional references and resources are given throughout. Sophisticated technology skills are not required. A special "Jump Start" page is offered for educators in a hurry. Developed by the National Staff Development Council and the Eisenhower National Clearinghouse, BYOD is exceptionally well designed and a major step forward in personalizing professional development.

16.5   Concept to Classroom
www.thirteen.org/edonline/concept2class/index.html

This collection of free, online workshops was prepared by New York City's PBS-TV station Channel Thirteen with the support of Disney. The workshops are very well designed and include leading experts in their respective fields. All workshops are self-paced and consist of sections devoted to "Explanation," "Demonstration," "Exploration," "Implementation," and "Get Credit." Generally, about 30–35 hours of work are expected to complete each workshop. All materials are available online including videos and handouts. In addition, each workshop is accompanied by a discussion area. The workshops have frequently been granted in-service credit by schools and districts.

Workshop titles: "Tapping into Multiple Intelligences"; "Constructivism as a Paradigm for Teaching and Learning"; "Teaching to Academic Standards"; "Why the Net?"; "Cooperative and Collaborative Learning"; "Inquiry-based Learning"; "Assessment, Evaluation, and Curriculum Redesign"; "WebQuests, Making Family and Community Connections"; "Interdisciplinary Learning in Your Classroom"; and "After-School Programs."

16.6   Issues Page: Professional Development
www.edweek.org/context/topics/issuespage.cfm?id=16

If you are just delving into the field of teacher professional development, this can be the best place to start. The page hosts an excellent essay, giving an overview of the topic. It also includes links to over a dozen current articles from *Education Week* dealing with the same topic, links to key vocabulary someone new to the field may need defined, and links to organizations that are active in the field. Finally, it also gives descriptions of numerous other spots on the web to expand one's knowledge and understanding of this area.

16.7   Knowledge Media Laboratory—Carnegie Foundation for the Advancement of Teaching
kml2.carnegiefoundation.org/html/gallery.php

The Carnegie Foundation is working to create new multimedia tools for K–12 and university teachers to imagine, document, and represent the scholarship of their teaching. Click "K–12" in the dropdown menu on the upper left side of this page. You are taken to a menu of selections in which teachers have created online documentation of student work, videos of their classrooms, and their reflections developed while teaching. These efforts capture deep ideas, insights, and new understandings generated in the course of teaching. The Knowledge Media Lab makes the work public so that others can build on it. This is an ambitious and groundbreaking initiative.

16.8 Looking at Student Work (LASW)
www.lasw.org

Developed by a core group of devoted individuals and organizations originally connected with the Chicago Learning Collaborative and the Annenberg Institute for School Reform, LASW proceeds from the premises that student work is serious, that it gives key data about the life of the school, and that the work of children and adults in schools should be public. LASW emphasizes focusing on small samples of student work, looking together at student work with colleagues, reflecting on important questions about teaching and learning, and using agreed-upon structures and guidelines for looking at and talking about student work. The site presents sample protocols for doing the work; books, articles, and videos; websites posting student work; links to websites giving practical examples; useful supporting tools; and research related to the approach.

16.9 National Staff Development Council (NSDC)
www.nsdc.org

NSDC provides a great set of tools for those who are responsible for staff development. The site contains several full-text, how-to books on professional development (including programs for administrators), a library of selected full-text articles and citations from its three periodicals, and links to other sites and organizations focused on professional development. Other good areas here are "Standards," the "Bookstore," and "Powerful Words" (which consists of a great many inspirational quotations).

16.10 "Realizing New Learning for All Students Through Professional Development"
www.ncrel.org/sdrs/areas/issues/educatrs/profdevl/pd200.htm

This is a nicely put-together policy guide for planning and implementing professional development programs. In addition to good advice on what to do, it offers action options and potential pitfalls. Notable is a series of audio interviews (with full-text transcripts) by leaders in the field including Linda Darling-Hammond, Beau Fly Jones, and Tom Davis. Key terms requiring definition or explanation are hyperlinked to pages providing the necessary information.

16.11 South Central RTEC—Video
www.southcentralrtec.org/products-6.html

These videos were produced to accompany the Active Learning with Technology package described in item 16.1. However, their use is not restricted to this program. They generally range from 14 to 20 minutes in length and are available in VHS (for sale), or for download (but users should have a fast connection or the download will take forever). The 10 titles include: "Engaged Discoverers: Kids Constructing Knowledge with Technology"; "Classrooms Under Construction: Integrating Student Centered Learning"; "Managing Growth"; "2nd Grade Classroom Episode: The Desert"; "Reading Buddies: 1st and 5th Graders Learning Together"; "4th Grade Bilingual Classroom Episode: Graphing"; "6th Grade Classroom Episode: Collaborative Language Arts"; "9th Grade Classroom Episode: Spanish Travelers"; "Authentic Algebra: Conics, Ellipses, and Parabolas"; and "Creative Geometry: CrossGrade Collaboration."

16.12 Teacher Professional Development
www.wested.org/cs/wew/view/top/24

WestEd is a nonprofit research, development, and service agency formed by the merger of two of the original federal Regional Educational Labs—the Far West Lab for Educational Research and Development with the Southwest Regional Lab. This page provides hotlinks to ten of WestEd's programs that are involved in teacher professional development, 69 of its projects that are involved with teacher professional development, and 83 of its resources that feature teacher professional development.

16.13   Teachers College of Western Governors University
www.wgu.edu/wgu/vu/teu/index.html

If online teacher education intrigues you, this Internet-based university may fit the bill. Those already holding a B.A. may accomplish all teacher certification or M.A. degree study online in WGU's competency-based curriculum, and then complete an in-person, six-month "demonstration teaching" period under the supervision of a classroom teacher. B.A. and Associate's degree programs are also offered.

Accredited programs at the Teachers College of WGU began in March 2003, and, according to the university, certification earned through it is transferable to 43 states based on currently existing reciprocity agreements. Programs for paraprofessionals have been designed to meet the new requirements of the No Child Left Behind act.

Degree and certificate programs are offered currently in Reading, Mathematics, and Technology at the elementary and secondary levels. Additional programs in Science, Bilingual Education, Mathematics, and Reading are planned to begin as early as the fall of 2003. Programs generally run from one to two years in length and currently are priced at approximately $2,250 per semester. Student loans and aid are available; enrollment begins the first of every month.

Chapter Seventeen

Projects

17.1   iEARN (International Education and Resource Network)
www.iearn.org

More than 135 international projects are featured here that focus on enabling young people to use the net and other technologies to participate in collaborations that both enhance learning and make a difference in the world. More than two dozen languages are used in various groups and projects. iEARN offers both online and in-person professional development to support the effective integration of standards-based, online global projects into classrooms. Samples of some projects include "Architecture and Living Spaces," "Celebrating Our Women," "Connecting Math to Our Lives," "Greensphere Project," and the "Global Teenage Project."

17.2   Global Schoolhouse (Global SchoolNet)
www.gsn.org

GSN focuses on international collaborative learning. It hosts a "Projects Registry" of more than 750 online collaborative projects, a Cyber-Fair (in its eighth year in 2003) in which students conduct research on their own communities to publish on the web, and "Online Expeditions" comprising many worldwide journeys. Other parts of the site include a "Classroom Conferencing" registry to encourage connections among classrooms worldwide; the "GeoGame" to help students learn about the world, its maps, and people; "Newsday" to help students create their own international student-written newspaper; "Professional Development" for educators; "Conversion Tools" to the best links for maps, language translators, measurement converters, currency and time zone converters, and postal zip codes; and "News and Discussion Lists."

17.3   The Best Projects Online

surfaquarium.com/IT/project.htm

A page of links to over 100 individual projects. Be sure to take a look at the "Collaborative Project Guidelines."

17.4   PBLnet.org (Project-Based Learning)

www.pblnet.org

Click on "Exemplary Projects" to locate 12 excellent interdisciplinary, standards-based projects designed for students in grades 5–8. When you reach the page listing these projects, click on "Other Great Projects" in the column on the left to find links to 18 more outstanding projects (grades 4–12). Subject areas include "Science and Invention"; "Media Arts and Media Literacy"; "Family, Oral and Community History & Folklore"; "Global Community Building and Intercultural Understanding"; "Music, Visual & Performing Arts"; "Cross Curricular"; "Mathematics"; and "Service Learning."

17.5   Telecollaborate!

telecollaborate.net

Here is a good spot whether you are just getting into online collaborative projects or are an experienced participant. For newcomers, Telecollaborate gives a "Participant's Guide," "Online Resources," and access to existing "Innovative Projects." For the more adventurous or experienced who wish to offer their own project, the site helps you "Assess Your Capabilities," "Design Your Telecollaboration," "Review Models," gives you "Tips for Leading a Successful Collaborative Project," and also access to software "Tools of the Trade." Online support and help are also available through e-mail.

17.6   WorldWatcher Project

www.worldwatcher.nwu.edu

"The WorldWatcher Project is dedicated to the improvement of Earth and environmental science education through the use of data visualization and analysis tools to support inquiry-based pedagogy. . . . Data visualization and analysis technologies . . . capitalize on the power of the human visual perception system to identify patterns in complex data."

Currently, WorldWatcher supports a stand-alone, eight-week Global Warming Project and a six-week Planetary Forecaster unit in which students investigate the major causes of global temperature variation. Both units are intended for grades 7–10 and are available without charge. Special software packages, called WorldWatcher and My World, are available for free download, as well as extensive curriculum support materials. A yearlong high school program called Looking At The Environment is also available by special arrangement. It is an inquiry-based, visually intensive environmental science course.

Chapter Eighteen

School Administration

18.1   About Learning
www.funderstanding.com/about_learning.cfm
   Brief descriptions of 12 leading theories on how people learn. Great for use with parents and community groups, also good for a quick personal brush-up. Topics include "Constructivism," "Behaviorism," "Piaget's Developmental Theory," "Neuroscience," "Brain-Based Learning," "Learning Styles," "Multiple Intelligences," "Right Brain/Left Brain Thinking," "Communities of Practice," "Control Theory," "Observational Learning," and "Vygotsky and Social Cognition."

18.2   An Educator's Guide to Schoolwide Reform
www.aasa.org/issues_and_insights/district_organization/Reform/index
.htm
   This 1999 report was prepared to analyze and assess 24 well-known whole school reform designs. The research was conducted by the American Institutes for Research and was supported by AASA, AFT, NAESP, NASSP, and NEA. Each design is thoroughly described, analyzed, and compared across six dimensions including "Evidence of Positive Effects on Student Achievement," "Year Introduced," "Number of Schools," "Extent of Developer Support Provided to Schools," and two aspects of "Costs."

18.3   *The Catalog of School Reform Models: Helping You Find the Right Model for Your School*
www.nwrel.org/scpd/catalog/index.shtml
   The Northwest Regional Education Laboratory and the National Clearinghouse for Comprehensive School Reform collaborated on this 2002

report that reviews 26 "Whole-School" reform models and 10 "Reading/Language Arts" models. Models are analyzed according to their general approach, results with students, implementation assistance, and costs.

18.4   Clearinghouse on Educational Policy and Management
cepm.uoregon.edu and also http://eric.uoregon.edu

This was the site formerly known as the ERIC Clearinghouse on Educational Management. It has transformed itself into CEPM in what appears to be a seamless manner. The site looks virtually unchanged and contains the same high-quality information. The most readily accessible resources are contained in the areas titled "Trends and Issues" and "Hot Topics." A sampling of topics addressed includes "Class Size," "Role of Local School Boards," "Student Motivation," "Scientific Research," "Whole School Reform," "Labor Relations," "Relationships with Community," "Role of the School Leader," and "School Choice."

18.5   Data-Driven Decision Making Tutorial
www.ncrel.org/toolbelt/tutor.htm

This program is part of a larger site called The ToolBelt: A Collection of Data-Driven Decision-Making Tools for Educators produced by the North Central Regional Educational Laboratory. The tutorial "introduces eight steps educators can take to begin using data to define their problems and needs, select improvement strategies and goals, initiate change, and evaluate their students' progress." The steps are "Develop a Leadership Team," "Collect and Organize Data," "Analyze Data Patterns, "Pose Hypotheses," "Develop Improvement Goals," "Design Specific Strategies," "Define Evaluation Criteria," and "Make the Commitment."

18.6   Data-Driven Decision Making: Vision to Know and Do
3d2know.cosn.org/index.html

The Coalition for School Networking (CoSN) launched this site to provide a clearinghouse for information on this essential topic. It includes a downloadable version of CoSN's important publication *Vision of Know and Do: The Power of Data as a Tool in Educational Decision Making*, case studies of best practices, a district self-assessment tool, copies of presentations on the topic, and a list of links to two dozen outstanding online resources.

18.7 Michigan Teacher Network—Educational Leadership
mtn.merit.edu/leader.html

The Michigan Teacher Network site represents a terrific effort to gather in one place "over 8,000 best practice, professional development, and standards-based resources." Among the many valuable items housed here, readers will find over 500 quality-reviewed websites in the "Educational Leadership" area. Resources are grouped into 12 subcategories such as "Assessment," "Community Outreach," "Human Resources," "Teacher Education," and "Urban School Issues." Make it a point to check the "Best Practices Information" as well.

18.8   Emerging Leadership Practices Inventory
www.ncrel.org/cscd/pubs/lead21/2-11.htm

This questionnaire focuses on self-assessment for school leaders in the context of building the school as a community of learners. It is a paper and pencil exercise that, once completed, will give you ample material for reflection.

18.9   High Schools That Work (HSTW)
www.sreb.org/programs/hstw/hstwindex.asp

HSTW, under the leadership of Gene Bottoms of the Southern Regional Education Board, is a very successful initiative that's active in over 1,000 middle and high schools in 23 states. For those who are not members of HSTW, the most useful parts of this website are "Background Information" (click on "Key Practices"), "Publications and Materials" (including three excellent PowerPoint presentations), "Professional Development" (see the "Guide for School Leaders"), "Assessment and Using Data," and "Outstanding Practices." Be sure to take a look at the "Case Studies in the Publications and Materials" section. They detail step-by-step how 14 different high schools have made significant progress in raising student achievement.

18.10   Institute for Educational Leadership (IEL)
www.iel.org

IEL publications will help almost any school leader. A full range of on-line reports is available. Individual titles are listed by the IEL program that issued them: *Coalition for Community Schools*, *IELeadership Connec-*

tions E-newsletter, *School Leadership for the 21st Century Initiative*, *Center for Workforce Development*, *IEL Policy Exchange*, *Systems Improvement Training and Technical Assistance Project*, *Other IEL Publications*, and *School-Family-Community Connections*.

Together with the Laboratory for Student Success at Temple University, IEL will soon launch a new website designed to help school districts "learn about sound principles of school leadership development content and design, and local exemplary leadership development programs, practices, and resources." As of this writing, the site is not yet active. Its URL will be www.e-lead.org.

IEL's home page features a hotlink to the 2003 Danzberger Memorial Lecture, given by Eli Broad, founder of the Broad Foundation. The lecture's provocative title is "School Boards: Part of the Problem or Part of the Solution?"

18.11   Leader to Leader Institute
www.l2li.org

This institute is devoted to strengthening leadership of the social sector—that certainly includes educators. It contains numerous free articles and links to other sites of interest to leaders. Many materials are also available for purchase. Major foci of the institute are on developing individual leadership and forging successful alliances between nonprofits and businesses.

18.12   Leadership Audit Tool—A Participatory Management Checklist
www.ncrel.org/cscd/proflead.htm

The focus of this 52-item questionnaire is assessing one's strengths and weaknesses in relation to skills of participatory management. After responding to the questions online, you can have your responses graphed for easy analysis.

18.13   Principals Electronic Desk
www.myped.net/index.vm

This is a neat, free service of the National Association of Elementary School Principals. It functions as an online magazine, giving regular updates in the following areas: "Community Relations," "Trends and Issues," "Technology Talk," "International Education," "Professional Development," "Middle School," and "Urban Schools." Online streaming audio interview excerpts are also part of this fine package. There are extensive archives of the interviews and all the articles. Check back periodically.

18.14   Statistics Every Writer Should Know—Robert Niles' Journalism Help
www.robertniles.com/stats

Not just writers, Robert; all of us in education need to know a little about stats too. This site is a great primer on the major topics you are likely to need from time to time. Quick, easy lessons are given for the math-averse in "Mean," "Median," "Percent," per capita, standard deviation, margin of error, "Data Analysis," and "Sample Sizes." "Stats Tests" offers helpful advice on what to do to insure the right statistical test is being used for the particular situation.

18.15   Teaching Methods/Subject Area Resources Links
www.mhhe.com/socscience/education/methods/resources.html

McGraw-Hill has produced a site that impresses me as an entire school of education on one website. It only provides links to other sites, but the way it is put together is so imaginative! The "Teaching Methods" section contains 21 topics, each with a selection of quality links. Some of the topics are "Scientific Basis for the Art of Teaching," "The Role of Planning in Teaching," "Curriculum Theory," "Learning Environments and Motivation," "Teaching of Concepts," "Problem-Based Learning and Instruction," "Creativity and Intelligence," and "Learning Strategies."

18.16   The Literacy Program Evaluation Tool
www.ncrel.org/literacy/eval

This is a systematic process, developed by the North Central Regional Educational Laboratory, for a building-level group to evaluate a school's literacy program. It asks key questions, provides information, and gives sample worksheets and checklists. Steps involved include "Establishing a literacy committee," "Building a knowledge base," "Conducting a needs assessment," "Formulating questions to focus the monitoring," "Organizing and analyzing information," and "Taking action." Look on the left side of the page for the link to "Literacy Research & Best Practices," which takes you to another of NCREL's outstanding collections of resources.

Chapter Nineteen

School and District Exemplary Websites

19.1   Ambleweb, Ambleside Primary School on the Web, Ambleside (Great Britain)

ambleweb.digitalbrain.com/ambleweb/web/home.db_psc

A remarkable collection of online learning resources for primary-aged students and their teachers from all over the world. This site has been online for so long, and proven to be so popular, that when it was revamped recently, the school had to give access to its old site as well as its new one! Navigate to "The Old Ambleweb" for archives of student work along with extensive resources on LEGO robotics, LOGO, technology integration at the primary level, lesson ideas, tutorials, and downloads—in English, French, German, Italian, Portuguese, and Spanish. The current site houses an incredible collection of online learning tools in all primary subjects in the "E-learning" area. Eight enjoyable online learning games appear in the "Games" section.

19.2   Athens District High School, Athens, Ontario

www.ucdsb.on.ca/athens

ADHS is located in a small, rural community in Ontario. The most notable feature of its website, which does not strive to offer a comprehensive view of the school, is the more than two dozen outstanding, student-produced web projects archived here.

19.3   Blue Valley Public Schools (Kansas)

www.bluevalleyk12.org

Blue Valley is a fairly sizable district (18,000+) in suburban Kansas City. The site is very instructive for parents and prospective residents—including a message from the superintendent and providing all the information one would expect regarding attendance, enrollment and health procedures, board information, curriculum, support services, and information for employees. Where Blue Valley excels is its communication functions and uses of data. BV InfoNet is an e-mail messaging service that provides members who sign up with timely information on topics affecting the schools and community. Voice messaging is provided for staff and parents. In addition, access to selected portions of the district's sophisticated Student Information System is presently being extended from staff to parents.

19.4   Centennial School, Lac du Bonnet, Manitoba, Canada
www.agassizsd.mb.ca/centennial

This K–6 school of about 300 students uses its website to emphasize communication and educational web links for students and teachers. Each classroom has its own pages full of news about what is happening and student work. The school also posts its monthly newsletter, staff list, major activities, calendar, and writing by student web reporters.

19.5   D. J. Montague Elementary School, Williamsburg, Virginia
www.wjcc.k12.va.us/djm

In this K–5 school, every teacher has a web page to inform students and parents. The home page houses dozens of links for student research, math, language arts, science, social studies, activity sites, tests, student work pages, teacher/parent links, and connections to the Williamsburg district, the Virginia State Department of Education, school lunch menus, schools calendars, a district map of school locations, and the PTA. In addition, links to favorite work and play sites for the computer lab are featured prominently. Finally, interested readers may take a virtual photographic tour of the school and its grounds. The site was designed by a high school student who graduated from Montague.

19.6   Greece Central School District (New York)
www.greece.k12.ny.us

Here is another very clean, informative, and easy-to-navigate school district site. Its crowning achievement is the area called "TASK" (Technology Advancing Student Knowledge). Find "TASK" by clicking on "Resources" in the lower right of the district start page. The "What's

New" area gives links to online tech magazines and other local tech news. "Internet Links" provides a hotlist of curriculum and teaching resources, organized by grade level and subject. "Teacher Tools" offers tips, tutorials, tools, and downloads. The jewel in the crown is the "Class Activities" area, which contains "technology enhanced activities and lesson ideas for teachers to use in their classrooms." It also includes samples of completed projects by Greece's own. Education World called "TASK" "the best in-house teacher resource ever."

19.7   Jefferson County Public Schools (Colorado)
jeffcoweb.jeffco.k12.co.us

If you have ever wondered what a school district can do to maximize use of the web for all of its clients (students, staff, parents, and community), this is the place to start your research. Modeled as a portal, Jeff-CoNet provides a dazzling array of services and information that is lightning quick, even on a dialup connection, and easy to navigate.

JeffCo was a leading technology district five years ago when I first encountered its presence on the web. Its site was exemplary then; now it is completely transformed . . . and even better. Any district that publishes a "Guide for School Webmasters" and an online newsletter for them has got to be thinking way ahead of the curve.

A great place to start looking around is JeffCoNet's "Communities" area, which offers separate sections for "Administrators," "Parents," "Librarians," "Secretaries," "Students," "Teachers," and "Counselors." The "Partners" area is unusual in that the district both hosts and links to a number of related community organizations. As JeffCo is the home of Columbine High School, the "Spirit of Columbine" section offers much to think about. Do not miss the "Teachers" community that offers incredible resources for any teacher, not just those within the district, including outstanding curriculum plans, online newsletters, links, and professional development. These folks are trailblazers!

19.8   Lawrence Public Schools (New York)
www.lawrence.org

It has won lots of awards. It is a little folksy. It is a little unusual. There is work by kids and lots of good web resources for staff. Anyone can sign up for the *EdTech Newsletter*. Each school has a web page that contains resources for students, teachers, and parents. Most of all, this site communicates that the district cares about the whole community and tries to offer information for everyone. Despite the fact that the system has only a little more than 3,000 students, its site shows that a few dedicated people can do a lot.

19.9   Northstar Elementary School, Knoxville, Iowa
www.nstarschool.com/welcome.htm

Wow! Without a doubt, this is the most visually clever and interesting school website I have ever come across. From a winking portrait of the President, to a working clock, calendar, and pull-down movie screen and map of the area, Northstar's web presence tells you that it is fun and chock full of good information. Every homeroom has its own home page, complete with buttons for events, student projects, links, parents, homework postings, games, and more. Many photos are included, along with a link to the district office. Parents can sign up for a daily e-mail from the school. It is also evident that the school still can grow into much of the site's functionality. Do not miss the "Educational Links." Come back here to see how this site evolves!

19.10   Oswego City School District (New York)
www.oswego.org

School district websites can be visually gorgeous and simple to use . . . this one proves it. Notable features include "Student Work," "K-6 Teacher Resources," and the "Photo Archive" of over 1,200 images produced by local students and staff. The district posts e-mail links to all faculty members and administration.

19.11   Tri-Valley Community Schools District #3, Downs, Illinois
tri-valley.k12.il.us

Check how this rather small (three schools) district has organized its home page to resemble an online newspaper. Current news assumes a prominent position, and every selection contains a contact for more information. Of course, school lunch menus can be located easily, and so can students' grades (privacy protected), daily announcements, and even directions to away games. The district raises funds through a very interesting SCRIP program with numerous local merchants, and teachers have access to a number of online administrative tools. Community members may access extensive information about the district and its operations. Tri-Valley achieves a rare level of transparency in how it goes about its business.

Chapter Twenty

Selected Strategies for Teaching

20.1   Ask an Expert Sites
k12science.ati.stevens-tech.edu/askanexpert.html
A comprehensive list of links to hundreds of ask-an-expert sites is found at this spot. Besides channeling you to 12 additional ask-an-expert directories, links are organized into categories including "Science and Math," "Medicine and Health," "Computing and the Internet," "History and Social Studies," "Economy and Marketing," "Professionals," "Personal and College Advisors," "Library Reference," "Literature and Language Arts," and "Just Out of Curiosity."

20.2   E-mail as a Springboard for Writing and Thinking
www.electronic-school.com/0398f5.html
www.iecc.org
www.epals.com
E-mail can be extraordinarily powerful in building your students' motivation, frequency, and fluency in writing as well as their thinking and composing skills. The first site listed here is an article I wrote that details 10 ways to seamlessly integrate use of e-mail penpals (called "keypals") into your academic program. The second and third sites are sources for finding online keypals, partner classes, and interactive collaborative projects.

20.3   Information Literacy
www.wlma.org/Instruction/infolit.htm
www.ccsd.edu/bardonia/CCSDLibraryCurriculum/hrdcpy/Final%20Draft1
.pdf

The need for students (and adults) to find, evaluate, and use success-fully the staggering amount of information available to them has never been greater. This is where programs in information literacy come in. The first of these sites, produced by the Washington Library Media Associa-tion, gives examples and links to several "Information Literacy Models" (including the model in widest use, "The Big 6"), "Sample Information Literacy Curricula," and "Practical Ideas for Teaching Information Liter-acy." The second site, produced by the Clarkstown Central School District in West Nyack, NY, consists of a complete "Information Literacy Cur-riculum, K–12." The document is based on national and state standards and provides clearly detailed references to them. Its lists of performance indicators at the elementary, middle, and high school levels are especially well done.

20.4   Lesson Study
www.teacherscollege.edu/lessonstudy/index.html
www.lessonresearch.net/index.html

Lesson study is a common professional development practice in Japan, where teachers work in groups to systematically develop, test, critique, and perfect lessons based on an overarching goal and related research questions they have decided to explore. The technique is gaining accept-ance and interest in the United States and other nations. These two sites, the first at Teachers College Columbia University and the second at Mills College, contain extensive readings, presentations, tools, samples, and links related to lesson study.

20.5   Virtual Field Trips
surfaquarium.com/IT/vft.htm
www.tramline.com

If you cannot take your class out into the world, bring the world to them. The Surfaquarium site gives links to over 100 of the best online field trips. On the Tramline site, you can use the company's software on a free trial basis to create your own virtual field trip, explore more than 30 free field trips, take an online workshop, visit an online tutorial, and purchase a hard-copy guide to "Using and Creating Virtual Field Trips."

20.6   WebQuests

www.techlearning.com/db_area/archives/WCE/archives/
webquwt.html

WebQuests could very well be the killer application for integrating the net into classroom instruction, right now. WebQuests are inquiry-oriented activities in which most or all of the information used by learners is drawn from the web. They are designed to use learners' time well, to focus on using information rather than looking for it, and to support learners' thinking at the levels of analysis, synthesis, and evaluation. Hundreds of Web-Quests are indexed here. This page consists of an article about Web-Quests, with links, that covers "What a WebQuest Is All About," "What Makes a WebQuest Worthwhile and Effective," "Some Tools to Construct a WebQuest," and "Further Reading and Interaction."

First developed by Bernie Dodge and Tom March at San Diego State University, WebQuests have grown tremendously in use and acceptance, and literally thousands are available online, as well as guidelines, templates, and rubrics devoted to their development, use, and evaluation. See Bernie Dodge's new site at webquest.org—it includes a great selection of the top current WebQuests. See also "Understanding and Using Web-Quests" at midgefrazel.net/lrnwebq.html and Tom March's new site, Best WebQuests, at www.bestwebquests.com.

20.7   Workshops by Thiagi

www.thiagi.com

Games and simulations can be powerful educational tools. While the ideal, comprehensive website on gaming and simulation has not been developed yet, this one has a lot going for it. The monthly newsletter is its strong point, available free by e-mail and archived back to June 2001. The issues contain sample simulation activities, tips for trainers (teachers), and interactive lectures.

Chapter Twenty-one

Teaching Resources

21.1 AOL@SCHOOL

www.aolatschool.com

AOL does a terrific job of sorting through all the web has to offer for education and organizing it in as user-friendly a way as possible. Resources are offered for students (grouped into primary, elementary, middle, and high school sections) and for educators (grouped into teacher and administrator sections). Each student section is further broken down into areas titled "Subjects," "Brain Teasers," "Study Kit," "Research and Reference," and "News and Current Events." "Daily Facts and Fun" changes every day.

The "Teachers" area includes a large collection of lesson plans, professional development resources, and classroom tools and tips, among others. The "Administrators" area includes sections on "Business Administration," "Operations," "Curriculum and Standards," "Library & Media," "Professional Development," and "Productivity Tools & Tips" among others.

Two especially useful sections of the site are the "Textbook Activities" area and "FFFBI" (The Fin, Fur, and Feather Bureau of Investigation). "Textbook Activities" takes the reader to supplemental online activities offered by textbook publishers to accompany all of their main series. This website allows the reader to search the free resources by textbook title, subject, or publisher. It is a very useful tool.

FFFBI, produced by the Boston's PBS-TV station WGBH, involves 8- to 12-year-olds in conducting investigations centered on contemporary global culture. Students engage in research to solve problems while they read, write, and think about topics in language arts, math, and science.

21.2   Children's Picture Book Library at Miami University
www.lib.muohio.edu/pictbks

Preschool to grade 3 educators, parents, librarians, and other professionals may use CPBL@MU as an efficient tool to design literature-based
thematic units for all areas of the curriculum. The searchable database
contains abstracts of over 5,000 picture books for children. Searches yield
numerous volumes with storylines that are adaptable and relevant to your
particular curriculum or program needs.

21.3   Copyright Bay
www.stfrancis.edu/cid/copyrightbay

Not only does Copyright Bay give you the latest information on the
complex field of copyrighted material in educational and nonprofit settings, it is instructional, visually interesting, self-correcting, and fun. It
consists of a self-instructional trip through "Fair Use Harbor," "Murky Wa-
ters," and "Infringement Reef." After reading introductory information on
a pertinent topic, you take a "Shakedown Cruise" to see if you can answer
hypothetical questions correctly. Correct answers are rewarded and incor-
rect ones are shown the proper way. It is a great model of the Internet as an
active instructional tool, not just a passive dispenser of information.

21.4   Creative Impulse
history.evansville.net/index.html

Kudos to Nancy Mautz—what a great achievement and obvious labor
of love. Ms. Mautz has created an organized and indexed set of links for
interdisciplinary study of the history and arts of Western civilization from
ancient times to the present. As she says, "I believe it is impossible to
properly study history without examining the creative products of the
times. The art, music, dramas, and literature of an age give us insight into
the minds and hearts of those who lived at that time. What better way to
view history than through the artist's eyes." Taking us on a journey
through the standard tour of the growth of Western civilization, we wend
our way from "Prehistory," "Mesopotamia," "Egypt," "India," and
"China," through "Greece" and "Rome," to the "Renaissance" and "En-
lightenment," and on to the ages of "Revolution," "Industry," and "Mod-
ern" and "Recent" times. In each area, sites are offered dealing with both
the history and the arts of the period.

In addition, Ms. Mautz has assembled a great alphabetical list of the history of more than 335 fascinating topics ranging from the "History of Acupuncture" to the "History of Zoos." These histories give annotated links to over 1,000 relevant sites.

21.5 DiscoverySchool.com
school.discovery.com

DiscoverySchool.com provides original resources for teachers, students, and parents. "Teaching Tools" features "Puzzlemaker" (to generate educational puzzles), "Lesson Planner" (to create and store your customized lesson plans), "Quiz Center" (to create and administer quizzes that are graded online, providing instant feedback to you and your students), and "Worksheet Generator" (to create custom worksheets). In "Custom Classroom," you can create and save your work in your own account. DiscoverySchool.com also supplies a great selection of "Brain Boosters," "Clip Art," and hundreds of original lesson plans that are indexed by grade level and subject and are fully searchable.

Of course, this site has a strong emphasis on the most powerful electronic medium at work today ... TV. Clips of programs are provided, along with schedules of upcoming broadcasts that are available for taping. The tips on using video in the classroom are excellent. Interested parties may sign up for regular e-mail updates and participate in online discussions.

21.6 Education World
www.education-world.com

Education World is a comprehensive and well put together portal for educators. It gives original articles, site reviews, a self-contained search engine, and lesson plans. The "Best Of" series details 20 top websites annually, going back to 1997. Original content includes articles for administrators, reports on new and interesting curriculum projects, news about schools, financial planning for educators, and educational technology use. The site also publishes e-newsletters including articles, updates, site reviews, job listings, news headlines, and education humor, and it maintains message boards in teaching, technology, the web, and administration.

21.7 EnGauge and 21st Century Skills
www.ncrel.org/engauge

www.metiri.com/features.html

www.21stcenturyskills.org

Do you know what skills the 21st century requires of today's learners? These companion NCREL and Metiri websites lay out an exceptionally well-documented case for a focus on "Digital Age Literacy," "Inventive Thinking," "Effective Communication," and "High Productivity." The NCREL site focuses on the relationship between high-performing school systems and the "21st Century Skills." The Metiri site gives an excellent summary pamphlet, the full *21st Century Skills* report, and cross-matches with other key skills sets. Take careful note of the document titled "Continua of Progress"; it is an outstanding set of rubrics for every one of the identified subskills. This is an outstanding achievement. Everyone concerned with the progressive education of our youth should become fully conversant with it.

Another group, called the Partnership for 21st Century Skills, used the 2003 NECC convention to launch its report titled *Learning for the 21st Century.* This group, composed of educators and business people, takes a position more directly related to the standards and assessment-driven NCLB act, to stake out its prospectus that emphasizes core subjects, learning skills, 21st-century tools, 21st-century context, 21st-century content, and 21st-century assessments. Their presentation is patterned after the influential work of the CEO Forum during the late 1990s in promoting technology penetration and integration in schools.

21.8   Humanities-Interactive

www.humanities-interactive.org/a_base.html

What a gem! The Texas Council for the Humanities Resources Center has produced this wonderful collection of "interactive exhibits, games, lessons," and additional resources.

More than 50 collections can be found here focusing on Texas and Mexican history and culture, ancient cultures, literature, "The New World," "Understanding Other Cultures," and "The Medieval World." Each of the exhibits, in addition to its fascinating collection of online artifacts, includes a teacher's guide, bibliography, interpretive essay, links to related quality-selected sites, and games for students. Some also include additional resources. Names of some of the exhibits include "The Treasures of Tutankhamun," "The Great Bronze Age of China," "Ice

Age Art," "Mexico: Splendors of Thirty Centuries," "Annexation: Celebrating 150 Years of Texas Statehood," "Literary East Texas," "Africa in the Americas," and "People's Lives: A Photographic Celebration of the Human Spirit."

21. 9   Indigenous Peoples Literature

www.indigenouspeople.net/ipl_final.html

This attractive site results from the obvious dedication of Glenn Walker. He has collected a rich array of resources devoted to indigenous people, most (but not all) from North, Central, and South America. Perhaps the most abundant resource is stories, followed by famous documents, quotes, poetry, music, and art. With a little digging, educators will be able to assemble excellent minicollections for use with students.

21.10   Innovative Teaching Newsletter

surfaquarium.com/NEWSLETTER.htm

For over six years, Walter McKenzie has regularly published an online and e-mail newsletter dedicated to thematic collections of websites for educators. Over 100 issues are archived here. Topics range from the "American Revolution" to "Back to School," "Mythology," "Physics," and "Women's History." It is a very useful set of collections.

21.11   Kathy Schrock's Guide for Educators

school.discovery.com/schrockguide

This is the zenith of all education websites that link to other sites; its breadth and depth are without peer—and it gets more user-friendly all the time. Kathy Schrock was a library media specialist at the Wixon Middle School in South Dennis, Massachusetts, and now serves as the Administrator for Technology for the Nauset Public Schools in Orleans, Massachusetts. Over 2,000 personally selected sites by Ms. Schrock are organized into 23 subject areas and alphabetically. "Sites of the School Days" offers ideas for technology integration, is published several times a month, and is archived back to 1999. Ms. Schrock's picks of the best content-rich sites are listed, and the Guide also publishes informational slide shows, links to sites on assessment, rubrics, and critical evaluation tools. Do not miss the "TeacherQuest" area where links to the author's "TechQuests" for classroom technology integration are archived monthly. Simply outstanding.

21.12   Marco Polo—Internet Content for the Classroom
www.marcopolo-education.org/home.aspx

Marco Polo combines online content and lessons from seven of the most outstanding providers on the net. One search of Marco Polo gives you connections to the best of the best. The monthly *MarcoGram* organizes resources into thematic curriculum units. These are archived on the site and can be sent to you by e-mail. Connections between Marco Polo lessons and standards from 30 states are indexed too. Extensive in-person and online "Professional Development" resources also constitute an important part of Marco Polo's mission. Trainer materials and handouts are easily accessible.

21.13   Media Literacy Review
interact.uoregon.edu/MediaLit/mlr/home/index.html

Here is an excellent twice-yearly e-journal for "educators and others interested in children, adolescents, and media." It contains informative articles and a truly outstanding collection of links. The first five issues of the journal have dealt with "Children and the Internet," "Nonfiction Film," "Kids Doing the Media," "Learning from Pictures," and "Radio and Youth."

21.14   Multicultural Pavilion: Resources and Dialogues for Equity in Education
www.edchange.org/multicultural/index.html

Paul Gorski has given us an exceptionally comprehensive compilation of materials on this vital subject. The start page takes you to the "Teacher's Corner," where you will see regularly updated features, classroom resources, literature, historic documents and speeches, children's literature, handouts, and tools. Other key areas of the start page include two research sections, multicultural songs, selected links, digital divide issues, community forums, and a listserv.

21.15   NASA Quest
quest.arc.nasa.gov

This site is a very user-friendly location for those interested in space and aviation. It supplies several live interactions with NASA experts each month, audio/video programs, lesson plans and student activities, opportunities for online student collaboration, background information and photo sections, a teachers' meeting place, a searchable FAQ with over 3,000 questions, and a personal e-mail question response service.

21.16   Plumb Design Visual Thesaurus
www.visualthesaurus.com/online/index.html

This spot will thrill and delight English teachers, writers, serious readers, and those who enjoy language. It takes the concept of a thesaurus, runs it through the Matrix, and deposits it in virtual 3-D for our learning and pleasure, just this side of Pixar and Dreamworks (well . . . maybe it is not quite that spectacular, but it is really cool). You may start by keying a word into the text field, but you will go very quickly to the "Guided Tour" in order to internalize the meaning of the fabulous information you receive. Its designers say the Visual Thesaurus "is both an artistic exploration and a tool to explore, study, and analyze the structure of language. By displaying the interrelationships between words and meanings as spatial maps, ... [it] translates language into a visible architecture." Amen; do spend some time here.

21.17   Project Gutenberg
www.promo.net/pg

Can't make it to the library to get a book? You might be able to read it online at Project Gutenberg, the net's oldest public archive of books. As of late 2002, nearly 6,300 full-text volumes were located at this place. You may browse lists by author or title. Most books either have an expired copyright and are in the public domain (many classics fall into this category) or are recently published e-books. Other great sites devoted to a similar purpose are Bartleby at www.bartleby.com and the Internet Public Library at www.ipl.org/div/books.

21.18   Resources on the Islamic World
cmcu.georgetown.edu/resources.html#research

In today's complex world, the need for authoritative information is critical. Georgetown University's Center for Muslim-Christian Understanding provides scholarly links to "Journals and Newspapers"; "Research Institutes and Organizations"; "University Programs"; "Teaching Resources"; "Publishers, Software and Music"; "Funding Agencies"; and "Societies and Associations"—all devoted to reliable information about Islam.

21.19   Science Fair Central
school.discovery.com/sciencefaircentral

Just as the name says, this spot is a crossroads for the science fair world. For students, it offers a comprehensive handbook on creating a project, a list of 50 project ideas in eight different areas, links and books to be used for research, a searchable database of over 300 science fair questions and answers, and tip sheets for "Astronomy," "Biology," "Chemistry," "Earth Science," and "Physical Science" projects. Teachers will find an organizer for planning a fair, and parents can use the tips for helping your young scientist.

21.20   TEAMS Distance Learning
teams.lacoe.edu

The Los Angeles County Office of Education has assembled this wonderful site, partially supported by a USDOE Star Schools grant. While part of the site is devoted to synchronous video-based instruction that is broadcast for KLCS-TV in Los Angeles, the asynchronous web portion is outstanding. Hundreds of quality-selected links are identified and described briefly in 27 categories. Some include "Classroom Projects," "Early Childhood Education," "History/Social Science," "Language Arts," "Mathematics," "Parent Resources," "Professional Development," and "Technology & Learning." Do not miss the link at the bottom of the home page titled "Electronic Classrooms." This particular collection of sites supplements TV programs in K–8 instruction. Each classroom in the hallway leads to more great links dealing with elementary mathematics, technology, science, social studies, literacy and language arts, and resources for parent involvement.

21.21   Teachers Network
www.teachersnetwork.org

Teachers Network is a nationwide, nonprofit organization that identifies and connects innovative public school teachers with one another. An outstanding feature provides free streaming video of exemplary classroom practices. The "New Teacher Helpline" is another great area that gives guaranteed responses to teacher questions within 72 hours. Additional resources are also offered, including online courses custom-designed for the new educator. "TeachNet" gives tips to integrate technology into the classroom, and hundreds of teacher-developed and approved lesson plans are located here too.

Teachers Network offers Impact II funding for new projects originated by teachers and also makes adopter grants to those wishing to replicate already funded ones. The site hosts several bulletin boards and enables you to order from the Network's excellent list of teacher-authored guides and publications. As if that were not enough, the Teachers Network Policy Institute provides teachers with a platform to bring their expertise and experience to current debates on education policy.

21.22 The Learning Page—Especially For Teachers
memory.loc.gov/learn

The Learning Page is designed for teachers to make the American Memory Collection at the U.S. Library of Congress more accessible and convenient in teaching American history and culture. "American Memory is an online archive of over 100 collections of rare and unique items important to America's heritage. The collections contain more than 7 million primary source documents, photographs, films, and recordings." The Learning Page comes with instructions for "Getting Started"; more than 50 lesson plans by grade level; "Feature Presentations" that gather together American Memory resources based on themes; specific activities; easy access to the 100+ collections; and extensive, hands-on resources for professional development.

21.23 ThinkQuest
www.thinkquest.org

No other site on the net comes close to illuminating the incredible talents of young people as does ThinkQuest. Designed as an annual competition among teams of young people who collaborate across distances to create web-based learning projects, ThinkQuest now houses a library of over 5,000 student-created websites that cover nearly every aspect of the school curriculum. ThinkQuest has gone international, so there are competitions, libraries, and other programs involving over a dozen nations, with separate collections of the work of elementary and secondary students, as well as teachers. The Internet Challenge Library organizes them by subject area and is searchable. You must visit the winners section, which compiles the best entries in multiple categories going back to 1996. The quality of the work will astound you!

21.24   YouthLearn
www.youthlearn.org

Do you work with youth and technology? If not, do you know someone who does? Here is a dynamite source of planning guides, teaching techniques, activities, and projects.

Samples of outstanding guides include: "Creating a Chapter Book," "A Video Project on Idioms," "Using Storyboards," "Teaching Visual Arts," "Teaching Media Literacy," "Teaching Computer Graphics and Image Editing," "Teaching Digital Photography," and "How to Create a Presentation." YouthLearn publishes a hard-copy practical guide to working with youth and technology and, in addition, a free online newsletter on best practices, lesson ideas, and grant sources that is archived on the site. The database of educational websites is very rich with teaching ideas and how-to pieces. "Excellent Planning Guides" give practical tools and advice on topics such as "Brainstorming Techniques," "Creating a Positive Climate," "10-Step Guide to Program Planning," and "Using Internet Lessons."

While aimed primarily at those who teach in after-school programs, YouthLearn is just as helpful to those who work with young people during school hours. Terrific samples of student work can also be found here.

Chapter Twenty-two

Technology in Support of Teaching and Learning

22.1   Apple Learning Interchange

ali.apple.com/ali_sites/ali/index.shtml

A great strength of the Apple Learning site is its use of video as a tool for demonstrating effective teaching and learning practices at all levels, pre-K–20. The "Exhibits" section provides ample evidence of successful practices. ALI also hosts a regular series of "Education Events" online and archives them on the site. Presenters in the series have included Bill Clinton, Bob Chase, Michael Fullan, and Rod Paige. A high-speed connection will make viewing the selections more efficient. Some "Virtual Field Trips" appear here, as well as an excellent, searchable collection of lessons that integrate the use of technology, called "Units of Practice."

22.2   CARET—The Center for Applied Research in Educational Technology

caret.iste.org

This CARET is not a vegetable, it is a goldmine—top quality research articles are summarized and indexed to give educational leaders the best possible sources for making technology decisions. Main topics addressed, all dealing with technology in education, include "Student Learning," "Curriculum and Instruction," "Online Teaching and Learning," "Professional Development," and "Assessment and Evaluation." The article database is searchable. Citations are given to additional research, case studies, and other resources. A great plus is that all reviewed articles, and the majority of the related research reports, are available online.

22.3   EduWeb—Educational Web Adventures
www.eduweb.com/index2.html

This company has developed numerous exceptional and award-winning, interactive, online learning websites involving art, history, and science. EduWeb possess an impressive client list of 30 institutions. Their sites are indexed by subject and by grade level. Those that have won major awards include "The Artist's Toolkit," "Kids Design Network," "ArtEdventures," "Jefferson's West," "Understanding Slavery," "A Brush with Wildlife," "Art Tales," "In Search of the Ways of Knowing Trail," "Arts Workshop," "Who's Out There? Searching for Extraterrestrial Intelligence," "A. Pintura: Art Detective," "Inside Art," and "Amazon Interactive."

22.4   George Lucas Education Foundation (GLEF)
glef.org

GLEF devotes itself to documenting and disseminating stories about exemplary practices in K–12 public education. Its EduTopia website offers extensive video selections and original text resources to serve its mission. The videos require a fast Internet connection to avoid long download times. The *GLEF Blast* e-mail newsletter delivers news, research, and inspiring stories twice a month. Major topics consist of "Innovative Classrooms," "Skillful Educators," and "Involved Communities." "Professional Development Modules" address "The Principal's Position," "Teacher Supervision and Development," "Project-Based Learning," and "Assessment." Each module includes articles, video, PowerPoint presentations, and class activities.

22.5   Handhelds
school.discovery.com/schrockguide/gadgets.html
www.handheld.hice-dev.org

With the use of handheld devices exploding in classrooms, the need for reliable information and guidance in their use has never been greater. The Schrock Guide site gives links to 11 Palm and Palm-type help sites, six recent articles, 10 sites on effective uses of digital cameras and camcorders, and 13 sites covering other devices. The Hi-CE site comes from the Center for Highly Interactive Computing at the University of Michigan, where pioneering work is being done on using handheld devices such as Palms as powerful educational tools. Hi-CE provides eight new free software applications for using Palms in the classroom, a free e-mail newsletter, and a number of message boards.

22.6 Homeschool World
www.home-school.com

Practical Homeschooling Magazine maintains Homeschool World as its online presence. HW gives dozens of articles from the magazine and lots of how-to advice for homeschoolers. Homeschool organizations from around the nation and the world are listed, and ask-an-expert bulletin boards are maintained for "Art," "Math," "Science," "Preschool," and "Unit Studies." Homeschool events around the country are listed, and on-line forums are hosted on topics such as "Getting Started," "Curriculum Trades," "Special Needs Homeschooling," "Homeschooling Overseas," "Military Homeschooling," and "Contests."

22.7 Internet Archive: Wayback Machine
webdev.archive.org/index.php

Have you ever looked for a website only to discover that it does not exist anymore? Here is hope for finding lost sites! The Internet Archive is working to gather and save as much of the current and the disappearing web as possible and make it available through the "Wayback Machine." As of early 2003, more than 10 billion pages had been stored. Just enter the URL for a site that has disappeared, and there's a great chance that "Wayback" will find it for you. My personal experience has yielded better than a 50 percent success rate.

22.8 Laptop Programs
www.learningwithlaptops.org
wireless.mivu.org/edcorner

Many schools and districts have seen the vision of a laptop for every student. Here is solid information about how to do it well. The first site, based on the experience of an independent school in Westchester County, New York, is fully searchable and offers "Latest News and Reports"; "Web Sites of Interest"; articles such as "Why Laptops?" "Guidelines for a Successful School Laptop Program," "Reflections on Laptop Program Implementation," and "Open Source Software"; and a listing of "Independent School Laptop Programs" across the nation. The second site documents ongoing efforts of the Learning Without Limits initiative in Michigan. To date, the state has spent over $10 million to eventually equip every student in Michigan with a wireless learning device. "Educator Corner" contains resources focused on "Best Practices," "Professional Development," and "E-learning Research."

22.9   Learning to Learn: Thinking and Learning Skills
www.ldrc.ca/projects/projects.php?id=26
    This free online course is for both able and (dis)abled young people and adults. It is designed to last for 10 weeks and "raise learners' awareness of the cognitive and metacognitive aspects of thinking and learning." With this awareness, learners will be better able to approach learning situations with flexibility and understanding how to adapt their strengths when needed. The course is available in French, Spanish, German, and English.

22.10   Learning with Technology
www.members.shaw.ca/priscillatheroux/images/default.html
    This location is a remarkable effort by one teacher in Canada to provide a comprehensive roadmap to the use of technology in education. It consists of excellent quotations on a variety of related topics, short summaries of research, and links to further resources. Topics include "Changing Attitudes," "Learning Strategies," "Teacher Resources," "Integrating Technology," "Integrating Outcomes," "Exploring Projects," "Sample Lesson Plans," "Planning Projects," "Thinking Skills," "Developing Web Pages," "Assessing," "Tutorials," and "Questions."

22.11   National Center for Technology Planning (NCTP)
www.nctp.com
    In keeping with the changing dynamics of the educational technology world, NCTP stays in motion too. On top of excellent resources for technology planning, the Center is expanding to include an emphasis on "Technology Auditing," with the planned addition of articles, resources, opinion pieces, and step-by-step aids for conducting an audit.
    NCTP's Tech Planning Guidebook (a guide for technology planning, as opposed to technology auditing) is now being published in version number 3.5. Links are given to "Ted Wesley's Technology-Based Needs Assessment Instrument," "Russell Smith's Needs Assessment Site," and

"Switched-On Classroom" published by the Massachusetts Software Council. Full-text samples of technology plans are posted for many states, districts, individual schools, universities, regions, cities, and even nations.

22.12   National Education Technology Standards Projects
cnets.iste.org

The International Society for Technology in Education's valuable tech standards for students, teachers, and administrators can all be found here. In addition to the standards themselves, these documents contain online resources, lessons and units, and profiles of exemplary practices. ISTE has also instituted a Distinguished Achievement Awards program for colleges and universities that do an outstanding job of implementing the teacher standards in their preservice preparation programs.

22.13   NICENET Internet Classroom Assistant (ICA)
www.nicenet.org

Do you yearn for a free, online collaborative workspace that is easy to use and contains no advertising? ICA is it! ICA features "Conferencing," "Scheduling," "Document Sharing," "Personal Messaging," and "Link Sharing." It is designed for educators to use with their classes, from elementary through graduate school, but any group can actually use the tools to participate in collaborative, online work. This spot lets you have virtual meetings! Private, password-protected spaces can be set up in minutes; there is no software to download; it works on any platform; and it was deliberately designed as a low-graphics environment to decrease page load time. See also the Tapped In site at www.tappedin.org for a similar free, online collaborative work environment.

22.14   One-Computer Classroom
facweb.furman.edu/~pecoy/mfl195/onecomputer.html

Many teachers work in classrooms containing only one, or just a few, computers. The idea here is that a one-computer classroom is a lot richer than one with none at all. When you are armed with these ideas and resources, you can maximize the situation and build a record of success to generate support for more technology in your room. This website compiles links to 79 other sites focused on the one-computer classroom that are organized into these categories: "PowerPoint Presentations Giving

Overviews," "Planning the One Computer Classroom," "Classroom Management," "Tips and Ideas for Using Technology," "Link Lists," and "Books."

Another good site on the same topic is One Computer Classroom Resources on the Internet at www.lttechno.com/links/onecomputerclassroom.html. Each link located here is described briefly.

22.15   Reviews of Education Software
www.evalutech.sreb.org

EvaluTech, maintained by the Southern Regional Education Board, exists as a searchable database of software, print sources, audiovisual resources, and websites in all subject areas and grade levels. All sources have been reviewed and quality-rated by panels of educators according to established criteria. Other tools located on this page include links to "Lesson Plans and Other Web Resources," "K-20 Online Learning," "Online Professional Development," and "Technology Resources for Students with Disabilities." Readers may also wish to consult www.evalutech.sreb .org/otherorgs/index.asp, which gives well-described links to "Other Organizations that Review Resources."

22.16   Teaching Teens to Teach (TTT)
www.americaconnects.net/research/FLOCCurriculum/FLOCCurriculum .asp

TTT was developed to create a cadre of instructors to lead technology training in community technology centers. The curriculum includes four modules and a video.

Module titles include: "Teaching Approaches and Techniques," "Effective Communication," "Project Management," and "Practicum in Teaching." Content, lesson plans, and activities are all included. While this material can readily be used to train teens to instruct in a variety of settings, including programs in which students train teachers, it can also be used to assist adult technology trainers.

22.17   techLEARNING.com
www.techlearning.com

Technology & Learning keeps going strong. This website companion to the print magazine goes far beyond what can be found on paper. Separate sections are maintained for teachers, tech coordinators, and administrators with a full archive of articles and annotated links. Four e-mail newsletters are published including *techLEARNING News* (with the Consortium for School Networking), *IT Guy Alert*, *Professional Development QuickTips Alert*, and *Site of the Day Alert*. *T&L* presents annual awards for outstanding software and websites that prove very useful year in and year out. Type "Awards of Excellence" into the search box to locate these award winners going back to the turn of the century (21st century, that is). See also *T.H.E. Journal* magazine at www.thejournal.com and its great collection of educational links called Educators Road Map at www.thejournal.com/highlights/roadmap/default.cfm.

22.18   Thirteen Ed Online
www.thirteen.org/edonline

This site is a truly comprehensive set of resources for educators; areas of the site are designed for educators, students (including adult learners), and parents/caregivers. Lesson plans provide original materials developed by selected educators. Eleven free teacher workshops occur online in topics such as "Constructivism," "Standards," "Assessment," "Cooperative Learning," and "After-School Programs." Each workshop comes with extensive resources and an excellent assessment rubric. A special "Video on Demand" section streams 1,400 K–12 videos for the classroom to New York state educators and residents. The National Teacher Training Institute gives even more training in video and Internet strategies and four online courses. An e-mail newsletter for educators provides TV broadcast updates and substantial classroom content.

22.19   Virtual High Schools
www.eclassroom.com/vhs/Post.html and www.eclassroom.com/vhs2003
www.edpath.com/research.htm
www.dlrn.org/k12/online.html

Distance learning is not confined to universities and continuing education. Virtual high schools, and even virtual elementary schools, are popping up all over the nation. In 2003, it was estimated that more than 50,000 K–12 students attended some kind of virtual school. The e-classroom site offers proceedings from an October 2002 conference called Building and Growing Your Online School: Successful Strategies for Real Results. The edpath site hosts two important California studies on this topic called *The California Virtual School Report* and *Summary of Proceedings from the Virtual High School Summer Institute 2002*. Within a great deal of related useful information, the dlrn site lists virtual high schools currently operating in the United States. These schools are sponsored by organizations as diverse as states, universities, school districts, charter schools, agencies and consortia, private nonprofits, and private for-profits.

22.20   ZD Net
www.zdnet.com

A major source of information for the technology world, ZD Net is divided into sections for "News," "Tech Update," "White Papers," "Reviews and Prices," and "Downloads." Despite its slant toward business, this spot offers a tremendous number of software downloads and the best reviews and price information on all things related to computers, peripherals, and software. All sections are searchable and indexed.

Chapter Twenty-three

Tutorials

23.1   AECT Prerequisite

aect.ed.psu.edu/viewlets/prerequisite.htm

AECT Prerequisite is part of the Association for Educational Communication and Technology's Project for Enhancing Learning Through Technology site. In this ambitious project, AECT is identifying the core technology skills teachers should possess for 46 different teaching roles, and will certify teachers who demonstrate them. AECT Prerequisite gives effective visual tutorials, in the form of applets, on 20 basic topics including "Computer Operations," "Networking," "Internet Knowledge," "Make a Web Page" (Dreamweaver and FrontPage), "Word Processing," "Spreadsheets," "Database Management," "Concept Mapping Software," "Graphics Design Software," "Developing Computer-Based Animation," "Scanning," "Converting Image Formats," "Using Digital Still and Video Cameras," "Email," "Using VHS Video Cameras," "Using a VCR," "Digitizing Video," and "Digitizing Audio."

23.2   Computers for Lunch (CFL)

www.discoverit.org/c4l

CFL is a great spot for beginners with technology, focused on elementary school. It is designed to be hands-on, activity-based, and self-instructional. What's more, each session is intended to take about 20 minutes, so teachers at lunch can spend a little time learning and still be able to have something to eat. Of course, you can work at your own pace anytime, anywhere, and the lessons will be helpful to adults and young people alike. Subjects include the web, e-mail, desktop publishing, creating web pages, tables and charts, graphics, and digital video. Instructional materials to use with students are also provided. CFL was developed at Simon Fraser University in British Columbia, Canada.

23.3   Microsoft Education Tutorials
www.microsoft.com/education/default.asp?ID=Tutorials

Microsoft's own tutorials, case studies, how-to articles, and lesson plans are organized into searchable pull-down menus organized by grade level, learning area, and Microsoft product.

23.4   Online Software Tutorials
www.liv.ac.uk/abe/students/tutorials.shtml

The University of Liverpool's School of Architecture and Building Engineering offers these 14 thorough tutorials. It is heavy on advanced graphics packages but also includes the very popular Director, Dreamweaver, Illustrator, Pagemaker, Photoshop, Premiere, and Publisher.

23.5   Online Classes—Learning Center
www.hplearningcenter.com

This site houses free, instructor-led online courses from Hewlett Packard. The growing collection of about two dozen courses is directed toward business users, but there is plenty for educators too. Some topics include "Using a Tablet PC," "Photoshop," "Creating PDFs," "Digital Photography," and "Dreamweaver."

23.6   On-Line Technology Tutorials
www.internet4classrooms.com/on-line2.htm

Hundreds of tutorials appear here, including the "MS Office Suite," "Graphics Applications," "Multimedia," "Operating Systems," "Internet and Web Page Development," "Integration" and much, much more. Do not miss the "On-line Practice Modules" link at the top of the page that opens up a whole new set of exercises designed for practice of software skills and applications. This is a solid job of compiling great links on an important topic.

23.7   TechTorials
www.education-world.com/a_tech/archives/techtutorials/index.shtml

Education World's TechTorials go beyond simply teaching you how to use software; they actually help you apply it to teaching tasks. More than two dozen examples include step-by-step guides on how to "Make a Countdown Clock," "Make a Timeline with Excel," and "How to Create a Web Page in 20 Minutes or Less."

23.8   TechTutorials

www.techtutorials.com

Now here is the hot spot for tech tutorial links for heavy hitters. It is tutorial world for everyone, not just educators. A constantly expanding and searchable list of nearly 2,000 tutorials covers "Applications," "BSD," "DOS," "Databases," "Handhelds," "Hardware," "Linux," "Macintosh," "Networking," "Novell," "OS2," "Programming," "Unix," "Webmaster," "Windows 2000," "Windows 9x," "Windows NT," and "Windows XP."

23.9   Workshop Handouts—Mississippi State University

www.its.msstate.edu/Information/Documentation/workshop.php

You will find workshop handouts and PowerPoint presentations here to help you learn and apply many of the most common applications for yourself or assist you to teach others. Topics include "Acrobat," "Illustrator," "PageMaker," "Photoshop," "Access," "Excel," "PowerPoint," "Network Video," "Operating Systems," "Statistics (SPSS)," "Web Development," and "Word Processing." You can locate additional handouts, PowerPoints, and exercises on building and maintaining websites with Flash, Dreamweaver, FrontPage, HTML, and JavaScript at www.its.msstate.edu/Information/Documentation/webdev_workshop.php.

Chapter Twenty-four

Urban Education

24.1   Alliance for Excellent Education
www.inclusiveschools.org

The Inclusive Schools site is devoted to improving urban schools through inclusive practices. The project is active in 11 districts such as Chicago, Clark County Nevada, Denver, Washington, D.C., Houston, Miami-Dade, Seattle, and New York (pending). The site offers an extensive searchable virtual library of resources such as books, articles, reports, and papers on thematic topics such as "Race and Ethnicity in Urban Schools," "Family and Community Life," "Inclusive Schools and Communities," "Systemic School Reform," and "School Climate and Classroom Environment." Numerous downloadable publications from the site include *Leadership Academy Manual*, *Districts on the Move*, and *Schools on the Move*.

24.2   Center for Effective Collaboration and Practice (CECP)
www.air.org/cecp

This center's mission is to improve services for children and youth with emotional and behavioral problems and to help communities create schools that promote emotional well-being, effective instruction, and safe learning. As our awareness of the destructive effects of stress in communities continues to grow, the resources offered by CECP assume increasing importance. "Issue Areas" address topics such as "Child Welfare," "Cultural Competence," and "School Violence Prevention and Intervention." Miniwebs give extensive research, discussions, and ask-an-expert access on topics such as "Functional Behavioral Assessment," "Prevention and Early Intervention," and "Strength-Based Assessment."

24.3   Center on Reinventing Public Education (CRPE)
www.crpe.org/index.shtml

CRPE, located at the University of Washington in Seattle, focuses its work on research and analysis devoted to urban school systems. All of the Center's work is available online. The site is divided into three sections: "Research," "Tools and Guides," and "New Ideas and Models." Information is intended primarily for educators, policy makers, and philanthropists.

24.4   Center for Research on Education, Diversity, and Excellence (CREDE)
www.crede.ucsc.edu

CREDE advocates "Five Standards for Effective Pedagogy" as a means to advance effective practices for excellence in teaching for all students, especially those at risk of educational failure due to cultural, language, racial, geographic, or economic factors. In summary, the five standards are "Joint Productive Activity," "Language and Literacy Development," "Contextualization/Making Meaning," "Challenging Activities," and "Instructional Conversation." Specific indicators are provided for each standard as well as video clips of each of the standards in action. Numerous reports and research briefs are available online or for purchase, along with many tools for teaching, professional development, research, and policy making.

24.5   Council of Great City Schools Online
www.cgcs.org

The Council is composed of 60 of the largest public urban systems in the United States. Its searchable site contains full text of most of the Council's reports in areas such as "Achievement Gaps," "Bilingual Education," "Professional Development," "Leadership and Governance," "School Finance," and "Indicators and Statistical Trends." "Promising Practices" summarizes presentations made at CGCS's annual conference. The Council's magazine, *Urban Educator*, is archived back to January 2001.

24.6   Perspectives on Urban Education
www.urbanedjournal.org

An online, refereed journal started in 2002 by the Graduate School of Education at the University of Pennsylvania. The first two issues contain a fascinating set of articles, presentations, and commentaries. Streaming videos of conference presentations made by some of the authors are a cool feature.

24.7 The Education Trust
www.edtrust.org

Ed Trust is devoted to high educational achievement by all students K–16, particularly those in institutions most often left behind. The site offers downloadable free copies of all recent publications in the *Thinking K-16* series as well as "Special Reports," and books. PowerPoint slides from selected presentations at Ed Trust's annual conference are also online. A prime feature here is Ed Watch Interactive, a user-friendly source of data on educational performance and equity by race and class, kindergarten through college, on a state-by-state as well as national basis.

Chapter Twenty-five

Young Children

25.1   Center for the Improvement of Early Reading Achievement (CIERA)
www.ciera.org

The two most useful parts of CIERA's site are its "Library" and the "Links." The "Library" is chock full of resources, reports, articles, and conference presentations. Based at the University of Michigan, CIERA is devoted to improving "the reading achievement of America's youth by generating and disseminating theoretical, empirical, and practical solutions to the learning and teaching of beginning reading."

25.2   EduPuppy
www.edupuppy.com

EduPuppy focuses on preschool through grade 2 education. It contains 53 indexed categories of resources. In addition, it enables users to create their own private web page of personal hotlinks. A selection of quality-approved products can also be purchased.

25.3   ERIC Clearinghouse on Elementary and Early Childhood Education
www.ericeece.org

During its existence, ERIC/EECE served as the best single location to access research and scholarly resources in its field. However, as indicated in the introduction to this book, federal support for this ERIC Clearinghouse has come to an end and the website has ceased to be active. Many of ERIC/EECE's resources are now housed at the Early Childhood and Parenting Collaborative (ECAP) at the University of Illinois.

Readers who go to the ERIC/EECE site will be directed to its more than 150 online research digests, 15 online book excerpts, most frequently requested information, and resources devoted to the Reggio Emilia Approach and the Project Approach. Some of this information is available in Spanish, Chinese, and Korean in addition to English. The bad news is that these great resources represent only a portion of what the former website contained, and what is no longer there may not be seen again (unless, of course, you access the old site through the Wayback Machine; see item 22.7).

Nevertheless, the good news is that hosting of the ERIC site by ECAP opens up additional sources of quality information on the education of young children. Log in to ECAP at ecap.crc.uiuc.edu/projects.html to access information on 15 early learning projects; the websites of 10 national, regional, and statewide centers hosted by ECAP; and 11 listservs focused on key issues related to young children's education. As a result of ERIC's demise, ECAP has now emerged as the best single source for information in this area.

25.4   iKnowthat
www.iknowthat.com

This is an interactive site for children ages 2–12, with numerous learning activities in writing, art, games, reading, and math. Information is available for parents to help in making selections. Children can create their own stories using backgrounds, text, characters, and sound effects. The games section helps children learn about physics and optics, and the reading section offers work in phonics and word games.

25.5   KizClub—Links
www.kizclub.com/link1.html

This portal gives entrance to some of the very best educational games on the web for young people. It contains the very highly rated Between the Lions, GameGoo, Starfall, FableVision, Storyplace, and Haringkids. A total of 24 games can be found on the four pages of links. They range in quality from good to great. The organization creating these games has partnered with some of the largest and most influential companies that focus on children (Disney, Scholastic, PBS, BBC, Riverdeep, Golden Books, and FisherPrice) to help add interactive, enjoyable learning to their sites.

25.6   Webbing into Literacy

curry.edschool.virginia.edu/go/wil/home.html

This site, based at the University of Virginia, focuses on Head Start. It stresses "a developmentally appropriate, balanced approach to literacy instruction, [and] provides teachers with guidance and suggestions for literacy development both in the classroom and at home." The program is based on nursery rhymes and the "101 Best Books from the Head Start Home-School Library." Teaching materials and activity cards are available online for use in school and at home. The basic approach focuses on a rhyme a week and a book a week.

About the Author

James Lerman designs educational environments and experiences for learners of all ages, from preschool through graduate school and beyond; particular passions of his include design, technology, politics, and the arts. He has been a classroom teacher, principal, staff development director, director of technology, assistant superintendent of schools, college professor, nonprofit executive, national conference presenter, consultant, founder of four new public schools, and author.